C++ game physics simulation

The complete guide to real-time physics simulation with C++

SIMON TELLIER

♦ Table of Contents

Part I: Fundamentals of Real-Time Physics Simulation

Creating a convincing real-time physics simulation is one of the most exciting and demanding challenges in game development. Before you can build a reliable physics engine or integrate realistic physical behaviors into your games, you need to master the essential foundations that govern how objects move, collide, and interact in a simulated environment. Part I of this book is dedicated to equipping you with those core building blocks.

Real-time simulation is all about balancing **accuracy**, **stability**, and **performance**. Unlike scientific simulations, where precision is the top priority, games require physics systems that are *fast* and *good enough* to create a believable world without overwhelming the CPU or GPU. Understanding this balance is critical — and it starts with a solid grasp of the underlying principles.

In this part, we will revisit the key elements of **Newtonian mechanics**, explore the **mathematics** that power transformations and rotations, and dive into **numerical integration methods** used to step physics forward frame by frame. You'll learn how forces translate into movement, how rotations are managed through matrices and quaternions, and why even small inaccuracies can snowball into major simulation problems if not handled properly.

Rather than overwhelming you with abstract theory, we'll focus on the ideas that matter most for real-world implementation. Each concept will be broken down in a way that bridges understanding and direct application in C++. Where complex math is involved, we will walk through it step-by-step, showing not only how the math works but how to turn it into working, efficient code.

By the time you complete Part I, you will have a rock-solid grasp of:

- The fundamental forces that drive physical behavior

- The mathematical tools needed for transformations, collisions, and rotations

- The practical ways to move simulated objects through time

Armed with these foundations, you will be ready to move on to the deeper systems of collision detection, contact resolution, and rigid body simulation, building steadily toward your own working physics engine.

Real-time physics may seem daunting at first glance — filled with complicated formulas, technical jargon, and tricky numerical methods — but at its heart, it's an elegant and intuitive framework. If you can understand how a ball bounces, how a car turns a corner, or how a spring stretches and recoils, you already have the instincts. Now it's time to build the knowledge and skills to bring those instincts to life in code.

Let's begin by stepping into the world of game physics — where the laws of motion come alive, one frame at a time.

Chapter 1: Introduction to Game Physics

Physics simulation is one of the most fascinating and essential aspects of modern interactive entertainment. It breathes life into static worlds, giving objects the ability to move, collide, and respond to forces in ways that feel natural to the player. Whether it's a character jumping over obstacles, a tower collapsing under its own weight, or a car skidding around a sharp corner, physics is at the heart of the experience.

In this chapter, we'll lay the groundwork for understanding game physics simulation. We will start by discussing what physics simulation actually means in the context of games, explore the critical role of physics engines, confront the unique challenges of real-time simulation, and conclude with an overview of how physics systems are built using C++.

By the end of this chapter, you'll have a clear perspective on why physics matters, how it shapes gameplay, and what lies ahead in building your own simulation systems.

1.1 What is Physics Simulation in Games?

At its core, physics simulation in games is the process of using mathematical models to mimic the behavior of physical objects in a virtual world. Unlike hand-animated movement, physics-driven motion responds dynamically to forces, collisions, and constraints — resulting in behavior that is emergent rather than pre-scripted.

When we talk about game physics, we are primarily referring to a few key areas:

- **Rigid body dynamics**: simulating solid objects like crates, balls, or vehicles that retain their shape when moving or colliding.

- **Collision detection and response**: determining when and how objects interact with each other and adjusting their motion accordingly.

- **Soft body physics**: simulating deformable objects like cloth, jelly, or flexible materials.

- **Particle systems**: managing groups of small objects like sparks, rain, or fluid droplets.

- **Constraints and joints**: connecting objects together with rules that limit their motion, like hinges or springs.

The goal of game physics isn't necessarily to create scientifically accurate simulations — it's to create *believable* behavior that feels consistent and intuitive within the game world. Players don't measure angles and forces with rulers; they react instinctively to how things move and behave. If the movement looks plausible and reacts logically to player input, the simulation succeeds.

Consider the difference between a ball that bounces when dropped and one that simply falls and stops. The bouncing ball communicates energy, elasticity, and a sense of fun. Players subconsciously appreciate the depth and realism that physics adds, even if they aren't explicitly aware of the complex math running under the hood.

In essence, physics simulation gives your virtual world *weight, inertia, and consequence*. It's what makes a world feel like it obeys rules — even if those rules are crafted selectively for gameplay purposes.

1.2 The Role of Physics Engines in Game Development

Because simulating physical behavior is computationally complex and critical to gameplay, developers typically rely on specialized software libraries called **physics engines**. A physics engine provides a reusable, efficient, and consistent way to manage the physical behavior of objects without reinventing the wheel for every project.

A physics engine typically handles:

- Managing the set of objects in the world

- Detecting collisions between objects

- Resolving contacts and applying appropriate forces

- Integrating motion over time (position, velocity, acceleration)

- Maintaining constraints between objects

Popular examples of full-featured physics engines include **Bullet, PhysX, Havok**, and **Box2D**. These engines are highly optimized, flexible, and capable of handling both simple and complex physical interactions in real time.

For indie developers, hobbyists, or those building custom game engines, understanding how physics engines work internally is invaluable. Even when using a third-party library, knowing the principles behind it enables you to configure, extend, and troubleshoot the system effectively.

Moreover, for certain specialized games — like those involving unusual interactions, highly stylized motion, or resource-constrained environments — developers often choose to build **their own lightweight physics systems**. This allows fine-grained control over performance, behavior, and integration with other parts of the game engine.

Physics engines can be broadly divided into two categories:

- **General-purpose physics engines**: capable of simulating a wide range of objects and interactions.

- **Domain-specific physics engines**: optimized for a particular type of simulation, such as vehicle dynamics, character ragdolls, or fluid flow.

Regardless of whether you are using a ready-made engine or building your own, understanding the architecture and operation of a physics simulation is essential for any serious game developer. In this book, we'll focus on constructing a flexible, practical foundation that can be expanded into a full custom engine if desired.

1.3 Challenges of Real-Time Simulation

Simulating physics in a game isn't as simple as plugging in the laws of motion and letting the math run wild. Real-time simulation brings with it a host of unique challenges that are very different from those encountered in scientific or engineering simulations.

Balancing Accuracy and Speed

In scientific computing, simulations often prioritize accuracy above all else, even if they take hours or days to complete. In a real-time game, however, every frame must be simulated and rendered in a few milliseconds — typically **under 16.6ms** for a smooth 60 frames per second experience.

This means physics calculations must be fast, predictable, and stable. Developers frequently have to simplify or approximate real-world physics to meet performance requirements.

For example:

- Collisions might be approximated using simple bounding shapes like spheres or boxes instead of detailed meshes.

- Forces might be integrated using faster, less accurate methods like semi-implicit Euler rather than complex, high-precision solvers.

- Very small or fast-moving objects might be ignored or merged into larger systems to avoid expensive calculations.

Stability and Error Accumulation

Numerical simulation inevitably introduces small errors. In a game environment, where hundreds or thousands of objects may interact simultaneously, these errors can accumulate and destabilize the entire simulation.

Common symptoms of unstable physics include:

- Objects slowly sinking into the ground

- Energy growing or dissipating unrealistically

- Objects jittering, vibrating, or exploding under stress

- Collisions being missed at high speeds (tunneling)

Techniques like **constraint stabilization**, **continuous collision detection**, and **energy conservation strategies** are critical to keeping simulations believable and stable over time.

Handling Complex Interactions

Games often involve complex interactions that are difficult to simulate cleanly:

- Stacks of objects need to balance without toppling from tiny errors.

- Moving platforms must interact correctly with carried objects.

- Characters need to walk, jump, and collide with uneven terrain.

- Destructible environments need to break apart convincingly.

Simulating these behaviors requires sophisticated systems for managing contacts, applying forces, and resolving motion constraints.

Debugging and Tuning

Unlike visual bugs that are often obvious, physics bugs can be subtle and difficult to reproduce. A small miscalculation in collision response might only show up once in a hundred playthroughs. Tuning parameters like friction, restitution, and constraint softness becomes a blend of science and art.

Building visual debug tools — to draw collision shapes, forces, and velocities — becomes essential for understanding what the simulation is doing internally and for tuning behavior.

1.4 Overview of Building Physics with C++

C++ is the dominant language for high-performance game development, and it is particularly well-suited for building physics systems thanks to its:

- **Fine-grained memory control**

- **High execution speed**

- **Strong support for mathematical abstractions**

- **Modern language features (C++17/20)** that enhance safety and expressiveness

Building a physics simulation with C++ typically involves creating a modular, extensible architecture that manages the following core concepts:

Representation of Physical Objects

Every simulated object needs:

- **Position and orientation** (typically using vectors and quaternions)

- **Linear and angular velocities**

- **Mass and inertia properties**

- **Collision shape and material properties**

Objects are often managed using *component-based architectures*, where different physical properties are attached to entities dynamically.

Force Application and Motion Integration

Each frame, forces (gravity, impulses, constraints) are accumulated, and the object's motion is updated by integrating acceleration to update velocity, and velocity to update position.

Choosing a stable, performant integration method — like semi-implicit Euler — is critical to ensuring that motion is smooth and believable.

Collision Detection

Collision detection typically happens in two stages:

- **Broad Phase**: Quickly eliminate pairs of objects that are too far apart to collide.

- **Narrow Phase**: Perform precise intersection tests between the remaining candidates.

Efficient collision algorithms are essential for scaling simulations to large numbers of objects.

Contact Resolution

When collisions occur, the simulation must:

- Determine the point of contact

- Calculate the collision normal and relative velocities

- Apply impulses to correct positions and velocities

- Enforce restitution and friction

This often requires solving small systems of equations to distribute forces realistically among contacting bodies.

Constraints and Joints

Constraints — like fixed joints, hinges, springs, and sliders — are added to restrict the motion of connected bodies. Solving these constraints requires careful mathematical handling to avoid simulation instability.

Optimization and Parallelization

As games become more complex, physics simulations must be optimized aggressively:

- Minimizing memory allocations

- Using SIMD instructions

- Parallelizing independent computations across CPU cores

- Reducing unnecessary calculations through smart scene management

By building systems modularly and carefully managing data flow, you can create simulations that scale from a few objects to thousands without degrading performance.

Physics simulation is both an art and a science. It demands a deep understanding of mathematics, careful engineering, and a relentless focus on performance and stability.

As you move forward in this book, we will build up each of these concepts step-by-step — always rooted in practical C++ code that you can run, modify, and extend.

Chapter 2: Mathematical Foundations for Simulation

When building any kind of physics simulation, math isn't just a helpful tool — it's the language the simulation speaks. Every position, velocity, collision, and rotation is described mathematically. Without a strong command of this language, creating believable real-time motion would be impossible.

Fortunately, the core mathematics needed for physics simulation are elegant, consistent, and surprisingly intuitive once you grasp them. In this chapter, we'll walk through the essential building blocks: vectors, dot products, cross products, matrices, transformations, rotations, quaternions, and coordinate frames.

You don't need a PhD in mathematics to build a working physics engine — but you do need to understand how to manipulate these structures correctly and efficiently, especially in the performance-conscious environment of C++ programming.

Let's start by laying the most important foundation: vectors.

2.1 Vectors, Dot Product, and Cross Product

Vectors

A vector is a mathematical object that has both a **magnitude** (length) and a **direction**. In physics simulation, vectors are used to represent positions, velocities, forces, accelerations, and almost anything involving movement or orientation.

In 3D space, a vector is typically represented as three components:

$v=(x,y,z)\mathbf{v} = (x,\ y,\ z)v=(x,y,z)$

These components define the vector's direction and how far it extends along each axis.

Key operations with vectors include:

- **Addition**: Combining two vectors (e.g., adding forces)

- **Subtraction**: Finding the vector from one point to another

- **Scaling**: Stretching or shrinking a vector by a scalar factor

- **Normalization**: Resizing a vector to have a magnitude of 1, preserving its direction

The magnitude (or length) of a vector $v\mathbf{v}v$ is calculated as:

$|v|=x2+y2+z2|\mathbf{v}| = \sqrt{x^2 + y^2 + z^2}|v|=x2+y2+z2$

Normalization is then simply:

vnormalized=$v|v|\mathbf{v}\_{\text{normalized}} = \frac{\mathbf{v}}{|\mathbf{v}|}$vnormalized=$|v|v$

This is crucial when you want a direction without caring about how long the vector is — for example, when calculating a unit force direction.

Dot Product

The **dot product** is a way of measuring how much two vectors point in the same direction. For vectors $a\mathbf{a}a$ and $b\mathbf{b}b$, the dot product is:

$a \cdot b=axbx+ayby+azbz\mathbf{a} \cdot \mathbf{b} = a\_x b\_x + a\_y b\_y + a\_z b\_za \cdot b=axbx+ayby+azbz$

14

The result is a single scalar value.

Properties:

- If the dot product is **positive**, the vectors point roughly the same way.

- If it's **zero**, the vectors are **perpendicular** (at 90 degrees to each other).

- If it's **negative**, they point in opposite directions.

In physics, the dot product is used for tasks like:

- Projecting one vector onto another

- Calculating angles between vectors

- Determining if a collision surface is facing a certain direction (e.g., for lighting or friction calculations)

The angle θ\theta$\theta$ between two vectors can be found via:

$\cos(\theta)$=a·b|a||b|\cos(\theta) = \frac{\mathbf{a} \cdot \mathbf{b}}{|\mathbf{a}||\mathbf{b}|}\cos(\theta)=|a||b|a·b

Cross Product

The **cross product** of two vectors results in a third vector that is **perpendicular** to both input vectors. For vectors a\mathbf{a}a and b\mathbf{b}b:

a×b=(aybz−azby, azbx−axbz, axby−aybx)\mathbf{a} \times \mathbf{b} = (a_yb_z - a_zb_y,\ a_zb_x - a_xb_z,\ a_xb_y - a_yb_x)a×b=(aybz−azby, azbx−axbz, axby−aybx)

The cross product is heavily used in physics for:

- Finding normals to surfaces

- Calculating torque (force applied at a distance)

- Determining rotational axes

The magnitude of the cross product represents the area of the parallelogram formed by the two vectors.

Understanding dot and cross products allows you to manipulate directions, detect alignments, and generate perpendicular forces — fundamental skills for real-time physics work.

2.2 Matrices, Transformations, and Rotations

While vectors represent directions and magnitudes, **matrices** represent **transformations** — ways of moving or rotating vectors.

In 3D, the most common matrix is a **4x4 matrix**, which can represent:

- Translation (moving an object)

- Rotation (spinning an object)

- Scaling (stretching an object)

- Any combination of the above

A typical 4x4 transformation matrix looks like:

[r11r12r13txr21r22r23tyr31r32r33tz0001]\begin{bmatrix} r_{11} & r_{12} & r_{13} & t_x \\ r_{21} & r_{22} & r_{23} & t_y \\ r_{31} & r_{32} & r_{33} & t_z \\ 0 & 0 & 0 & 1 \end{bmatrix}r11r21r310r12r22r320r13r23r330txtytz1

Where:

- The top-left 3x3 portion handles rotation and scaling

- The rightmost column (tx,ty,tz)(t_x, t_y, t_z)(tx,ty,tz) handles translation

Transforming a Vector

To apply a transformation matrix to a vector, you multiply the matrix by the vector (extended to a 4-component vector with a 1 appended).

This operation allows you to:

- Rotate vectors around arbitrary points

- Move objects through space

- Chain multiple transformations together efficiently

Rotation Matrices

A rotation matrix is a specialized 3x3 matrix that rotates vectors around an axis. For example, a rotation around the Z-axis by an angle θ\theta$\theta$ would look like:

$$\begin{bmatrix} \cos(\theta) & -\sin(\theta) & 0 \\ \sin(\theta) & \cos(\theta) & 0 \\ 0 & 0 & 1 \end{bmatrix}$$

Rotation matrices must be:

- **Orthogonal**: rows and columns are unit vectors

- **Determinant = 1**: preserves volume and shape

Incorrect handling of rotation matrices leads to distortions, artifacts, or numerical drift over time — a critical reason why understanding them deeply is essential.

2.3 Understanding Quaternions for 3D Rotations

While matrices can handle rotations, they have drawbacks:

- They can become numerically unstable.

- They suffer from **gimbal lock** (loss of one degree of freedom during rotation).

To overcome these issues, game developers use **quaternions** for rotations.

A quaternion is composed of four components:

$$q = w + xi + yj + zk$$

or more compactly:

$$q = (w, x, y, z)$$

Quaternions encode a rotation around an arbitrary axis in 3D space.

Advantages of Quaternions

- No gimbal lock

- Smooth interpolation between rotations (slerp - spherical linear interpolation)

- Compact and efficient storage (only four numbers)

- Fast and stable concatenation of multiple rotations

How Quaternions Work

Given a rotation of angle θ around a unit axis vector (x, y, z), the quaternion is:

$$q = \left(\cos\left(\frac{\theta}{2}\right), x\sin\left(\frac{\theta}{2}\right), y\sin\left(\frac{\theta}{2}\right), z\sin\left(\frac{\theta}{2}\right)\right)$$

To apply the rotation to a vector:

1. Convert the vector into a quaternion with w=0.

2. Perform the operation $v' = qvq^{-1}$, where q^{-1} is the conjugate of the rotation quaternion.

3. Extract the vector part of the result.

In practice, libraries handle much of this math behind the scenes, but understanding it empowers you to implement your own systems, debug problems, and optimize performance.

2.4 Coordinate Systems and Frame Transformations

A **coordinate system** defines how points are located in space relative to an origin and set of axes.

In games, you frequently switch between:

- **Local Space**: coordinates relative to an object

- **World Space**: coordinates relative to the overall world

- **Camera Space**: coordinates relative to the camera view

When simulating physics:

- Forces like gravity are usually in world space.

- Forces from motors or joints may be defined in local space.

- Collisions often require converting points between spaces.

Frame Transformations

Frame transformations involve changing the point of reference:

- To convert from **local space** to **world space**, multiply by the object's transformation matrix.

- To convert from **world space** to **local space**, multiply by the **inverse** of the transformation matrix.

Handling these conversions correctly ensures forces, velocities, and collisions behave consistently across the simulation.

2.5 Essential Linear Algebra Tools in C++

In C++, handling these mathematical operations efficiently is key to building a responsive physics system.

You typically define lightweight, high-performance classes for:

- **Vector3** (for 3D vectors)

- **Matrix4x4** (for transformation matrices)

- **Quaternion** (for rotations)

Each class should support:

- Operator overloading (e.g., +, -, *, /) for natural syntax

- Inline math functions to avoid function call overhead

- Optimized memory layouts for SIMD acceleration

- Explicit construction and conversion routines

For example, a simple Vector3 class might look like:

cpp

CopyEdit

```cpp
struct Vector3 {
    float x, y, z;


    Vector3() : x(0), y(0), z(0) {}
    Vector3(float x_, float y_, float z_) : x(x_), y(y_),
z(z_) {}


    Vector3 operator+(const Vector3& other) const {
        return Vector3(x + other.x, y + other.y, z +
other.z);
    }


    Vector3 operator*(float scalar) const {
```

```
    return Vector3(x * scalar, y * scalar, z * scalar);

}


float dot(const Vector3& other) const {

    return x * other.x + y * other.y + z * other.z;

}


Vector3 cross(const Vector3& other) const {

    return Vector3(

        y * other.z - z * other.y,

        z * other.x - x * other.z,

        x * other.y - y * other.x

    );

}

};
```

By building these classes carefully, you lay the groundwork for all the higher-level physics systems to come.

Physics simulation is built on a firm mathematical foundation. Mastering vectors, matrices, quaternions, and coordinate frames gives you the tools to describe any motion, any rotation, and any force interaction you can imagine.

Chapter 3: Newtonian Mechanics Refresher

At the heart of any physics simulation lies the timeless framework of Newtonian mechanics. These are the laws that govern how objects move, interact, and respond to forces in the world around us — and in our simulated environments.

In real-time physics engines, Newton's principles are used not with scientific rigor but with practical effectiveness. They form the intuitive bridge between mathematical abstractions and the behavior players expect when they toss a ball, crash a vehicle, or swing from a rope.

This chapter revisits the essential concepts of forces, mass, acceleration, energy, work, momentum, and rotational dynamics. It also looks at how natural forces like gravity, drag, and friction are modeled in simulations. Whether you're refreshing old knowledge or learning these ideas anew, understanding them is critical for building solid, reliable game physics.

Let's begin with the basics — the relationship between force, mass, and acceleration.

3.1 Forces, Mass, and Acceleration

Force is a push or pull that changes an object's motion. In the real world, forces are everywhere: gravity pulls objects down, muscles push and pull limbs, engines drive cars forward.

Newton's Second Law of Motion describes the core relationship:

$$\mathbf{F} = m\mathbf{a}$$

Where:

- $\mathbf{F}$ is the force vector

- m is mass (scalar)

- $\mathbf{a}$ is acceleration vector

This simple equation is the beating heart of physics simulation. It tells us that the acceleration of an object is directly proportional to the force applied and inversely proportional to its mass.

In practical simulation:

- To apply a force to an object, you compute the resulting acceleration: $\mathbf{a} = \mathbf{F} / m$.

- Then, you integrate acceleration to update velocity and position over time.

Mass and Its Role

Mass is a measure of how much an object resists changes to its motion. In simulations:

- A **larger mass** object will accelerate more slowly under a given force.

- A **smaller mass** object will respond quickly to the same force.

Importantly, mass affects **both linear motion and rotational motion**, though rotational effects involve the more complex concept of **moment of inertia** (discussed later).

Many physics engines allow specifying an **inverse mass** value instead of mass itself. This avoids division during force calculations — multiplying by the inverse mass is faster and more stable than dividing by mass at runtime.

If an object is immovable (infinite mass), its inverse mass is zero.

Accumulating Forces

Throughout each simulation frame:

- Forces are **accumulated** on objects (gravity, impulses, collisions, user controls, etc.).

- At the physics step, all forces are summed and applied to compute the final acceleration for that frame.

Good engine design often uses a **force accumulator** system, clearing all forces after each simulation step.

cpp

CopyEdit

```cpp
void RigidBody::applyForce(const Vector3& force) {

    accumulatedForces += force;

}
```

Then during the physics update:

cpp

CopyEdit

```
Vector3 acceleration = accumulatedForces * inverseMass;

velocity += acceleration * deltaTime;

position += velocity * deltaTime;

accumulatedForces = Vector3(0, 0, 0);
```

This structure ensures that forces from multiple sources combine naturally each frame.

3.2 Energy, Work, and Momentum

Beyond simple force and acceleration, a deeper understanding of energy, work, and momentum brings greater control and nuance to a simulation.

Work and Energy

In physics:

- **Work** is the transfer of energy via force over distance.

- **Energy** is the capacity to do work.

Work is defined as:

$$W = \mathbf{F} \cdot \mathbf{d}$$

Where $\mathbf{d}$ is the displacement vector. Work is positive if the force acts in the direction of motion and negative if it opposes it.

Two major forms of energy relevant to simulations are:

- **Kinetic Energy** (energy of motion):

$$KE = \frac{1}{2}mv^2$$

- **Potential Energy** (stored energy, e.g., gravity):

$$PE = mgh$$

where h is height above a reference point.

In an ideal, frictionless world, the total mechanical energy (kinetic + potential) of a system remains constant. In games, energy often dissipates — through friction, collisions, or user inputs — but understanding energy conservation helps prevent unrealistic behavior like perpetual motion.

Momentum

Momentum is the quantity of motion an object has:

$$\mathbf{p} = m\mathbf{v}$$

In collisions:

- Momentum tends to be conserved.

29

- Colliding objects transfer momentum to one another.

Simulations use momentum calculations to determine how objects bounce off each other or absorb impacts.

When resolving collisions, you calculate the **impulse** needed to correct velocities so that momentum and (optionally) energy are conserved according to material properties (restitution, friction).

Impulse is the integral of force over time, but in real-time physics, it's typically applied as an instantaneous correction during the collision resolution phase.

3.3 Angular Motion and Rotational Dynamics

Translational motion is only half the story. Realistic physics simulations must also account for how objects rotate — how they spin, wobble, and respond to torques.

Rotational Equivalents

Rotation has equivalents for all the quantities we've discussed so far:

Translational Concept	Rotational Analog
Force (F)	Torque (τ)
Mass (m)	Moment of Inertia (I)

Acceleration (a)	Angular Acceleration (α)
Velocity (v)	Angular Velocity (ω)
Position (p)	Orientation (Quaternion or Matrix)

Torque

Torque is the rotational equivalent of force. It causes changes in rotational motion and is calculated as:

$$\tau = \mathbf{r} \times \mathbf{F}$$

Where:

- $\mathbf{r}$ is the vector from the center of mass to the point of force application

- $\mathbf{F}$ is the force vector

- $\times$ denotes the cross product

Moment of Inertia

The **moment of inertia** describes how much an object resists changes to its rotation, depending not just on mass but how that mass is distributed relative to the axis of rotation.

For simple shapes:

- Solid Sphere: I=25mr2I = \frac{2}{5}mr^2I=52mr2

- Solid Box: I=112m(l2+w2)I = \frac{1}{12}m(l^2 + w^2)I=121m(l2+w2)

Complex objects require tensor calculations, but for many games, approximate inertias based on simple shapes suffice.

Angular Equations of Motion

The rotational analog of Newton's Second Law:

τ=Iα\mathbf{\tau} = I\mathbf{\alpha}τ=Iα

Where:

- τ\mathbf{\tau}τ is torque

- III is moment of inertia

- α\mathbf{\alpha}α is angular acceleration

In simulation:

- Accumulate torques each frame

- Update angular velocities

- Update object orientations via quaternions or rotation matrices

The process mirrors linear motion but with a few added complexities around angular math stability.

3.4 Gravity, Drag, and Friction Models

Realistic simulations aren't just about pure motion — they must account for everyday forces like gravity, air resistance, and friction, which are vital for believable dynamics.

Gravity

Gravity is simple to model and ubiquitous in games. It is a constant downward force applied to all dynamic objects.

In Earth-like conditions:

$$F_{gravity} = m\mathbf{g}$$

Where $\mathbf{g}$ is typically $(0, -9.81, 0)$ meters per second squared.

Gravity is usually added as a continuous force every frame.

cpp

CopyEdit

```cpp
applyForce(Vector3(0, -9.81f * mass, 0));
```

Some simulations modify gravity for stylistic reasons — adjusting its strength or direction to match gameplay needs.

Drag (Air Resistance)

Objects moving through a fluid (like air) experience a force opposing their motion, called **drag**.

Drag force can be approximated as:

Fdrag=−kdv\mathbf{F}_{drag} = -k_d \mathbf{v}Fdrag=−kdv

Where kdk_dkd is a drag coefficient and v\mathbf{v}v is velocity.

This linear model is simple and effective for games. Higher drag values make objects slow down faster when moving through air, water, or other resistive mediums.

For more realism (e.g., at high speeds), a quadratic model is used:

Fdrag=−kd|v|v\mathbf{F}_{drag} = -k_d |\mathbf{v}|\mathbf{v}Fdrag=−kd|v|v

This accounts for how drag increases with the square of speed.

Friction

Friction is the force resisting sliding between two surfaces in contact.

There are two major types:

- **Static Friction**: Prevents initial motion

- **Dynamic (Kinetic) Friction**: Resists ongoing motion

Dynamic friction force:

Ffriction=−μdN\mathbf{F}_{friction} = -\mu_d NFfriction=−μdN

Where:

34

- μ_d\mu_d$μd is the dynamic friction coefficient

- NNN is the normal force (usually equal to mgmgmg on flat surfaces)

Friction is handled during collision resolution by adjusting the tangential velocities at contact points.

Correct friction modeling makes surfaces feel appropriately sticky, slippery, or somewhere in between — critical for character movement, vehicle tires, or sliding puzzles.

Mastering forces, energy, momentum, and rotational dynamics sets the stage for building powerful, believable simulations. Realistic object behavior starts here, with the simple but profound rules Newton laid out centuries ago — rules that, with the right mathematical tools and coding techniques, you can now bend and shape to create dynamic, engaging worlds.

Chapter 4: Time Integration Methods

In physics simulation, understanding forces and motion is only half the battle. Once you have calculated the forces acting on an object, you need to use them to update the object's position and velocity over time. This process — moving an object forward through small increments of time — is called **numerical integration**.

Unlike continuous systems described by calculus, digital simulations work with discrete steps. At each frame, you must approximate how the system changes based on the information available. The better your integration method, the more stable, accurate, and believable your simulation will be.

In this chapter, we will explore the fundamentals of numerical integration, examine popular methods such as the explicit Euler, semi-implicit Euler, and Runge-Kutta techniques, and discuss how to choose the right integrator depending on your game's needs.

By the end of this chapter, you'll have the tools to advance any physical system smoothly and reliably through time — one frame at a time.

4.1 Introduction to Numerical Integration

In a perfect mathematical world, solving motion under forces would involve solving differential equations analytically — finding exact solutions for position and velocity over time.

In real-time simulations, that's rarely practical or even possible. Instead, we approximate the solution over very small time steps using **numerical integration**.

The basic idea is simple:

- Given the current state of an object (position, velocity, etc.)

- And the forces or accelerations acting on it

- Compute the new state after a small timestep Δt\Delta tΔt

Over many tiny timesteps, these approximations produce motion that appears continuous and natural.

However, the method you choose for integration has a huge impact on:

- **Accuracy**: How closely the simulated path matches the true path

- **Stability**: How resistant the simulation is to numerical errors and chaotic behavior

- **Performance**: How much computation is needed each frame

Choosing the right method — and understanding its tradeoffs — is critical to building a responsive, believable physics system.

4.2 Explicit Euler and Semi-Implicit Euler

The simplest and most widely used integration methods are variations of **Euler integration**. Though simple, they can be surprisingly effective when used wisely.

Explicit Euler

The **explicit Euler method** is the most straightforward approach:

1. Compute the acceleration from the current forces.

2. Update the velocity based on acceleration.

3. Update the position based on the old velocity.

Formally:

$$v(t+\Delta t)=v(t)+a(t)\Delta t \quad \mathbf{v}(t+\Delta t) = \mathbf{v}(t) + \mathbf{a}(t)\Delta t$$
$$v(t+\Delta t)=v(t)+a(t)\Delta t \quad p(t+\Delta t)=p(t)+v(t)\Delta t \quad \mathbf{p}(t+\Delta t) = \mathbf{p}(t) + \mathbf{v}(t)\Delta t \quad p(t+\Delta t)=p(t)+v(t)\Delta t$$

Where:

- v $\mathbf{v}$ v = velocity

- p $\mathbf{p}$ p = position

- a $\mathbf{a}$ a = acceleration

- Δt Δt Δt = timestep

Advantages:

- Extremely simple to implement

- Very fast computation

- Easy to understand and debug

Disadvantages:

- Poor stability with large timesteps

- Can gain or lose energy artificially

- Prone to spiraling errors over time

In practice, explicit Euler is fragile. It's usually only acceptable for small systems, slow-moving objects, or when using very tiny timesteps.

Semi-Implicit (Symplectic) Euler

A slightly modified form, often called **semi-implicit Euler** or **symplectic Euler**, addresses many of explicit Euler's problems by flipping the order of updates:

1. Update velocity based on acceleration.

2. **Use the updated velocity** to update the position.

Formally:

v(t+Δt)=v(t)+a(t)Δt\mathbf{v}(t+\Delta t) = \mathbf{v}(t) + \mathbf{a}(t)\Delta tv(t+Δt)=v(t)+a(t)Δt p(t+Δt)=p(t)+v(t+Δt)Δt\mathbf{p}(t+\Delta t) = \mathbf{p}(t) + \mathbf{v}(t+\Delta t)\Delta tp(t+Δt)=p(t)+v(t+Δt)Δt

Notice the subtle but crucial difference: you're using the new velocity immediately, rather than the old one.

Advantages:

- Better energy conservation

- More stable over large timesteps

- Still simple and fast

Disadvantages:

- Still an approximation; not perfectly accurate

- Can cause small but noticeable artifacts in some cases

In real-world game physics, **semi-implicit Euler** is often the best compromise between stability, speed, and simplicity — making it a popular choice for many engines.

Quick Implementation Example

cpp

CopyEdit

```cpp
void integrateSemiImplicitEuler(RigidBody& body, float
deltaTime) {
    if (body.inverseMass == 0.0f) return; // Static objects
don't move

    // Apply forces to acceleration
```

```
    Vector3 acceleration = body.forces * body.inverseMass;

    // Integrate velocity
    body.velocity += acceleration * deltaTime;

    // Integrate position
    body.position += body.velocity * deltaTime;

    // Clear forces
    body.forces = Vector3(0, 0, 0);
}
```

This compact structure is at the heart of many simple physics engines.

4.3 Runge-Kutta Methods (RK2, RK4)

For more demanding simulations — where high stability and accuracy are required — developers often turn to **Runge-Kutta methods**.

Runge-Kutta methods improve upon Euler by taking multiple intermediate samples within a timestep, blending them together to produce a better estimate of the final state.

RK2 (Midpoint Method)

The **second-order Runge-Kutta method** (RK2) — sometimes called the **midpoint method** — improves accuracy by:

1. Taking an initial velocity and position.

2. Estimating a midpoint using a half timestep.

3. Using the midpoint acceleration to update velocity and position.

Pseudocode structure:

cpp
CopyEdit

```cpp
Vector3 midpointVelocity = velocity + 0.5f * acceleration *
deltaTime;
Vector3 midpointPosition = position + 0.5f * velocity *
deltaTime;

Vector3 midpointAcceleration =
computeAcceleration(midpointPosition, midpointVelocity);

velocity += midpointAcceleration * deltaTime;
position += midpointVelocity * deltaTime;
```

RK2 is **much** more stable than simple Euler, with only a modest increase in computational cost.

RK4 (Classic Runge-Kutta)

The **fourth-order Runge-Kutta method** (RK4) is a heavy-duty technique that takes four samples per step and blends them with carefully chosen weights.

The idea is to:

- Sample the system's behavior at the start, halfway, and end of the timestep.

- Combine these samples to predict the final state.

The formal RK4 algorithm is slightly complex but offers **very high accuracy** — often used in engineering and scientific simulations.

Advantages:

- Excellent accuracy and energy conservation

- High stability even with larger timesteps

Disadvantages:

- Computationally expensive

- Overkill for many fast-paced, interactive games

In real-time games, RK4 is often unnecessary except in niche cases like orbital simulations, complex articulated vehicles, or VR applications demanding ultra-smooth motion.

4.4 Choosing the Right Integrator for Games

With multiple integration methods available, how do you choose the right one for your project?

It depends on several factors:

- **Complexity of the simulation**: More complex or precise systems benefit from better integrators.

- **Performance constraints**: Faster methods leave more CPU time for graphics, AI, etc.

- **Timestep size**: Small timesteps mitigate instability even with simple integrators.

- **Gameplay needs**: Does perfect realism matter, or just plausible behavior?

Here's a practical rule of thumb:

Situation	Recommended Integrator
Simple 2D games, casual mobile games	Semi-Implicit Euler
3D physics with moderate stability needs	Semi-Implicit Euler or RK2
Highly precise simulations (space games, VR physics)	RK2 or RK4
Physics with very large timesteps	RK2 or better

Many commercial engines — including those powering major AAA titles — still rely primarily on **semi-implicit Euler**. When paired with small timesteps (like 1/60 or 1/120 seconds) and robust collision handling, it provides excellent real-time results with manageable CPU costs.

If you encounter instability (jitter, energy gains, exploding simulations), consider:

- Reducing timestep size

- Switching to a better integrator (like RK2)

- Adding damping, friction, or constraint stabilization mechanisms

Choosing and tuning your integrator is a vital part of the simulation pipeline — a subtle yet powerful influence on how the world feels and responds to player interaction.

Physics simulation in games is ultimately an art of compromise: between precision and speed, between stability and chaos, between perfect realism and playful engagement.

By mastering time integration, you unlock the ability to move your simulated world forward — smoothly, believably, and under your control.

With motion integration understood, we are now ready to tackle the next major system: **collision detection**, the art of making objects aware of — and responsive to — each other.

Part II: Core Systems for Realistic Simulation

With a strong understanding of fundamental physics principles and time integration techniques, it's time to dive deeper into the systems that form the backbone of a realistic simulation. Part II focuses on the essential components that allow objects to not just move through space, but interact with each other and the environment in meaningful, believable ways.

Realistic simulation demands more than isolated motion. It requires careful management of how objects detect collisions, how those collisions are resolved, how forces are distributed through contact points, and how complex interactions like stacking, sliding, and bouncing are handled without instability.

In this section, we will explore the inner workings of collision detection algorithms, contact resolution strategies, and rigid body dynamics. You'll learn how to build fast and robust systems that can manage thousands of moving parts without breaking down under computational stress. We'll also look at how physical properties like mass, restitution, and friction shape the way objects respond to the world and to each other.

By the end of Part II, you will have the knowledge needed to design and implement the critical infrastructure that underpins every great physics-driven game — the systems that make virtual worlds feel solid, alive, and governed by consistent rules.

Now, let's begin with the first and perhaps most crucial of these systems: collision detection.

Chapter 5: Collision Detection Fundamentals

In any real-time physics simulation, collision detection is one of the most critical — and computationally demanding — systems. Without an efficient collision system, objects would pass through each other, float endlessly in space, or behave in ways that instantly break the player's immersion.

Collision detection ensures that the virtual world feels solid and responsive. When two objects should meet, the simulation must detect their interaction quickly and precisely, providing information necessary for appropriate response — bouncing, sliding, or halting movement altogether.

In this chapter, we'll explore how collision detection systems are structured, starting with broad phase and narrow phase separation, then diving into bounding volumes, basic algorithms, and advanced spatial partitioning techniques.

By mastering collision detection, you'll be able to create simulations that scale efficiently and remain stable even with complex interactions involving dozens, hundreds, or even thousands of objects.

5.1 Broad Phase vs Narrow Phase Detection

Collision detection can be thought of as a two-step process:

Broad Phase

The broad phase is about **eliminating obvious non-collisions quickly**. Rather than checking every possible object against every other object — a process that grows exponentially with the number of objects — the broad phase uses fast, simple tests to filter out object pairs that are too far apart to possibly collide.

Typical broad phase strategies include:

- Bounding boxes or spheres

- Spatial partitioning (grids, trees)

- Sweep and prune algorithms

The goal here isn't accuracy — it's **speed**. A broad phase culls the vast majority of object pairs with minimal computational effort.

Narrow Phase

Once potential colliding pairs have been identified by the broad phase, the **narrow phase** takes over. The narrow phase performs **detailed, precise collision tests** between the shapes involved, determining:

- Whether an actual collision occurred

- Where the collision occurred (contact points)

- How deep the overlap is (penetration depth)

- The normal vector at the collision point

The narrow phase must be accurate because its results feed directly into the collision response system that determines how objects react physically.

Together, the broad and narrow phases ensure that the collision detection system remains both fast and precise — critical for real-time performance.

5.2 Bounding Volumes: AABB, OBB, Sphere Colliders

Bounding volumes are simplified geometric shapes that "wrap" around objects, providing fast approximations for collision tests.

AABB (Axis-Aligned Bounding Box)

An AABB is a box that aligns with the world's coordinate axes. It's defined by two points: the minimum and maximum corners.

Advantages:

- Extremely fast to test for overlap.

- Simple to compute and update (especially if objects are static or move predictably).

Disadvantages:

- Not tight-fitting for rotated objects.

- May be overly conservative for complex or rotated shapes.

An AABB collision test is as simple as checking whether the ranges along each axis overlap.

OBB (Oriented Bounding Box)

An OBB is similar to an AABB, but it **rotates with the object**. It's defined by a center point, a set of local axes, and extents along those axes.

Advantages:

- Tighter fit for rotated or irregular objects.

- More accurate broad phase results.

Disadvantages:

- More expensive to compute collisions (requires projections onto arbitrary axes).

OBB testing usually involves more complex mathematics, often relying on the Separating Axis Theorem (covered later).

Sphere Colliders

A sphere collider is simply a sphere defined by a center point and radius.

Advantages:

- Fastest collision test possible (distance check).

- Rotation has no effect — a sphere looks the same from every angle.

Disadvantages:

- Poor fit for non-spherical objects.

Sphere-sphere collision detection involves calculating the distance between centers and comparing it to the sum of their radii.

5.3 Axis-Aligned Bounding Box Collision Algorithms

Because AABBs are so simple, they form the backbone of many collision detection systems, especially during the broad phase.

AABB vs AABB Overlap Test

To check if two AABBs overlap, you perform a simple test on each axis (X, Y, Z):

- If they are separated along any axis, they **do not collide**.

- If they overlap on all axes, they **do collide**.

Pseudocode example:

cpp
CopyEdit
```cpp
bool aabbOverlap(const AABB& a, const AABB& b) {
    return (a.max.x > b.min.x && a.min.x < b.max.x) &&
           (a.max.y > b.min.y && a.min.y < b.max.y) &&
           (a.max.z > b.min.z && a.min.z < b.max.z);
}
```

This test is incredibly fast — just a few comparisons per object pair — making it ideal for broad phase culling.

Updating AABBs

If objects are moving, their AABBs must be updated every frame:

- For simple translations, just offset the min and max points.

- For rotations, you may need to recompute the box to fully enclose the rotated shape, often resulting in a slightly larger AABB.

Optimizing AABB updates is crucial for maintaining performance when many objects are in motion.

5.4 Separating Axis Theorem (SAT) for Polygons

For more complex shapes — especially **convex polygons** and **polyhedra** — the **Separating Axis Theorem** (SAT) provides a powerful collision detection method.

The Core Idea

SAT states that two convex shapes **do not intersect** if there exists an axis along which their projections **do not overlap**.

In practice:

- Find potential separating axes (normals to edges or faces).

- Project both shapes onto each axis.

- Check for gaps in the projections.

If a gap is found on **any axis**, the shapes are not colliding. If no gaps are found on all axes, the shapes are colliding.

Applying SAT

For 2D polygons:

- Test the normals of all edges from both polygons.

For 3D polyhedra:

- Test face normals from both shapes.

- Test cross products of edges between the shapes.

SAT provides:

- Collision status (yes or no).

- Penetration depth and collision normal (for response).

Though more computationally intensive than AABB tests, SAT offers tight, reliable collision detection for arbitrary convex shapes — critical for games with complex rigid body interactions.

5.5 Spatial Partitioning Techniques (Grids, Trees)

Even efficient pairwise tests can become overwhelming with hundreds or thousands of objects. To scale simulations, we use **spatial partitioning** — organizing space into regions so we only check collisions between nearby objects.

Uniform Grids

The world is divided into a regular grid of cells. Each object is inserted into the cells it overlaps.

Advantages:

- Very fast insertion and lookup.

- Good for uniformly distributed objects.

Disadvantages:

- Wasted memory if the world is mostly empty.

- Poor efficiency with highly dynamic or unevenly distributed objects.

Quadtrees and Octrees

Hierarchical structures where space is recursively divided into smaller regions:

- **Quadtree** for 2D (divides into four child nodes).

- **Octree** for 3D (divides into eight child nodes).

Objects are inserted into the smallest node they fit within.

Advantages:

- Efficient handling of uneven object distribution.

- Scales well for sparse or clustered environments.

Disadvantages:

- More complex insertion and management.

- Performance can degrade if objects move rapidly between nodes.

Sweep and Prune

Objects are sorted along one or more axes based on their bounding volumes:

- Pairs are generated by sweeping through the sorted list and checking for overlaps.

Advantages:

- Very fast when objects move slowly (minimal resorting needed).

- Well-suited for static or semi-static worlds.

Disadvantages:

- Less effective for highly dynamic scenes where object order changes drastically every frame.

Collision detection is a vast and fascinating field. Building a scalable, responsive system involves balancing speed, accuracy, and computational cost at every level — from the simplicity of AABB tests to the robustness of SAT and the efficiency of partitioning schemes.

With collision detection mastered, we are now ready to address the next major challenge: **collision resolution** — turning overlap detection into realistic physical responses.

Chapter 6: Contact Resolution Techniques

Detecting that two objects are overlapping is only the first half of solving collisions. To create a believable, stable simulation, you must also **resolve** these collisions correctly — meaning you have to calculate how objects react when they collide: how they bounce, slide, come to rest, or move apart.

This is the task of **contact resolution**. Done well, it makes the world feel solid, responsive, and physically plausible. Done poorly, it leads to jittering, sinking, popping, or exploding objects — quickly breaking player immersion.

In this chapter, we'll cover the essential techniques for handling collision response: applying impulses to correct velocities, correcting penetration, modeling bounce with restitution, and simulating friction for sliding and sticking behavior.

These techniques are the foundation of every robust real-time physics engine.

6.1 Impulse-Based Collision Response

At the moment of collision, two objects exert forces on each other. Instead of modeling these forces over real time (which would require complex and expensive calculations), we approximate the interaction with an **impulse** — a sudden, instantaneous change in momentum.

An impulse directly modifies an object's velocity without dealing with force integration over time.

Basic Impulse Response

When two objects collide:

- They apply equal and opposite impulses to each other.

- The impulses are aligned along the **collision normal** (the direction from one object to the other at the point of contact).

The basic impulse calculation is:

j=−(1+e)(vr·n)1ma+1mbj = -\frac{(1 + e)(\mathbf{v_r} \cdot \mathbf{n})}{\frac{1}{m_a} + \frac{1}{m_b}}j=−ma1+mb1(1+e)(vr·n)

Where:

- jjj = impulse scalar

- eee = coefficient of restitution (controls bounciness)

- vr\mathbf{v_r}vr = relative velocity at contact point

- n\mathbf{n}n = collision normal (unit vector)

- ma,mbm_a, m_bma,mb = masses of the two objects

Once jjj is computed:

- Apply jnj\mathbf{n}jn to one object (adding to its velocity).

- Apply −jn-j\mathbf{n} −jn to the other object (subtracting from its velocity).

Pseudocode:

cpp

CopyEdit

```cpp
Vector3 relativeVelocity = bodyB.velocity - bodyA.velocity;

float velocityAlongNormal = dot(relativeVelocity,
contactNormal);

if (velocityAlongNormal > 0) {

    // Objects are separating, no impulse needed

    return;

}

float e = min(bodyA.restitution, bodyB.restitution);

float j = -(1 + e) * velocityAlongNormal;

j /= bodyA.inverseMass + bodyB.inverseMass;

Vector3 impulse = j * contactNormal;

bodyA.velocity -= impulse * bodyA.inverseMass;

bodyB.velocity += impulse * bodyB.inverseMass;
```

This simple system gives convincing bounce, sliding, and sticking behavior when tuned carefully.

Why Use Impulses?

- **Efficiency**: No need for expensive force integration during contacts.

- **Stability**: Immediate correction avoids overlap stacking.

- **Flexibility**: Easy to add effects like friction and restitution adjustments.

Impulse-based collision response is the industry standard for real-time games because it balances simplicity, speed, and realism beautifully.

6.2 Penetration Depth Correction

Collision detection often happens **after** objects have already overlapped slightly — especially with discrete-time simulations. Left unchecked, this penetration can accumulate over time, leading to objects sinking into the ground or passing through each other.

To fix this, we apply **penetration depth correction**.

Positional Correction

After detecting a collision:

- Measure the **penetration depth** (how far the objects overlap).

- Move the objects apart along the collision normal by a small amount proportional to the penetration depth.

Typically, the correction is shared between the two objects based on their masses (lighter objects move more).

Simple correction:

cpp

CopyEdit

```cpp
const float percent = 0.8f; // 80% correction

const float slop = 0.01f;   // Allow small penetrations

float correctionMagnitude = max(penetrationDepth - slop,
0.0f) / (bodyA.inverseMass + bodyB.inverseMass);

Vector3 correction = correctionMagnitude * percent *
contactNormal;

bodyA.position -= correction * bodyA.inverseMass;

bodyB.position += correction * bodyB.inverseMass;
```

Key details:

- A **small slop** value prevents over-correction and jittering from tiny numerical errors.

- Correction is typically applied **before** applying velocity impulses.

Baumgarte Stabilization

More advanced systems integrate positional correction directly into the velocity solver, applying small corrective velocities instead of explicit position shifts. This method, known as **Baumgarte stabilization**, improves energy conservation but is trickier to tune.

For most games, simple post-collision positional correction works well and is easy to implement.

6.3 Restitution: Modeling Bounciness

Not all collisions should behave the same way. A rubber ball should bounce vigorously; a lump of clay should barely rebound. This property — the ability to bounce — is governed by **restitution**.

Coefficient of Restitution

Restitution is a value between 0 and 1:

- **0** = perfectly inelastic (no bounce)

- **1** = perfectly elastic (maximum bounce)

The coefficient determines how much velocity is preserved along the collision normal after impact.

In the impulse formula:

j=−(1+e)(vr·n)1ma+1mbj = -\frac{(1 + e)(\mathbf{v_r} \cdot \mathbf{n})}{\frac{1}{m_a} + \frac{1}{m_b}}j=−ma1+mb1(1+e)(vr·n)

The eee term directly scales the impulse to account for energy loss or retention.

Typically:

- Each object has its own restitution value.

- The collision uses the **minimum** restitution of the two colliding objects to prevent unexpected energy gains.

Example:

cpp

CopyEdit

```
float e = min(bodyA.restitution, bodyB.restitution);
```

Tuning Restitution

Realistic values depend on the materials being simulated:

- Rubber ball: 0.80.80.8

- Wood block: 0.30.30.3

- Metal object: 0.60.60.6

- Lump of clay: 0.00.00.0

Setting restitution carefully can dramatically affect the "feel" of your game's world — making it feel light, heavy, energetic, or deadened as needed.

6.4 Friction Forces and Sliding Behavior

While impulses and restitution handle collisions along the collision normal, real-world objects also experience **friction** — a force that resists sliding along contact surfaces.

Without friction:

- Objects would slide forever after collision.

- Stacks of objects would constantly slip apart.

- Characters and vehicles would be uncontrollable.

Thus, adding friction is essential for realism.

Static and Dynamic Friction

There are two types of friction:

- **Static friction**: resists initial motion when objects are at rest.

- **Dynamic (kinetic) friction**: resists ongoing sliding motion.

In games, friction is often approximated with a simple **Coulomb friction model**.

Given:

- μ_s\mu_sμs = static friction coefficient

- μ_d\mu_dμd = dynamic friction coefficient

- NNN = magnitude of normal force (collision impulse)

Apply friction impulse:

1. Calculate relative tangential velocity (velocity minus normal component).

2. Compute desired friction impulse opposing this tangential motion.

3. Clamp friction impulse based on normal impulse scaled by friction coefficients.

Pseudocode:

cpp

CopyEdit

```cpp
Vector3 relativeVelocity = bodyB.velocity - bodyA.velocity;

Vector3 tangent = relativeVelocity - (dot(relativeVelocity,
contactNormal) * contactNormal);

tangent = normalize(tangent);

float jt = -dot(relativeVelocity, tangent);

jt /= bodyA.inverseMass + bodyB.inverseMass;
```

65

```
float mu = sqrt(bodyA.friction * bodyB.friction); //
Combined friction

// Clamp friction impulse

Vector3 frictionImpulse;

if (abs(jt) < j * mu) {

    frictionImpulse = jt * tangent;

} else {

    frictionImpulse = -j * mu * tangent;

}

bodyA.velocity -= frictionImpulse * bodyA.inverseMass;

bodyB.velocity += frictionImpulse * bodyB.inverseMass;
```

This simple model captures most of the important behavior players expect:

- Objects slow down when sliding.

- Stacks resist sliding until pushed hard enough.

- Different materials interact naturally (ice vs rough ground).

Tuning Friction

Like restitution, friction coefficients should be tuned based on materials:

- Ice: $\mu d \approx 0.05$\mu_d \approx 0.05$\mu d \approx 0.05$

- Metal: $\mu d \approx 0.2$\mu_d \approx 0.2$\mu d \approx 0.2$

- Rubber: $\mu d \approx 1.0$\mu_d \approx 1.0$\mu d \approx 1.0$

Proper tuning ensures the world behaves intuitively and consistently.

Collision resolution brings your simulated world to life — determining not just if objects interact, but how they interact: with bounce, slide, stickiness, and dynamic energy exchange.

By mastering impulses, penetration correction, restitution, and friction, you create a foundation for building robust, realistic, and responsive simulations.

In the next chapter, we will dive even deeper into the physical modeling of objects themselves — exploring **rigid body dynamics**: how to simulate full-bodied motion with rotation, inertia, and torque.

Let's continue.

Chapter 7: Rigid Body Dynamics in C++

Rigid body dynamics are at the heart of realistic game physics. While simple motion and collision detection handle many basic interactions, true physical realism demands accounting for how solid objects move, spin, and interact based on mass, shape, and applied forces.

Rigid body simulation adds a crucial dimension to gameplay immersion. Instead of objects feeling like floating points or unbreakable blocks, they behave as tangible entities — capable of rolling, tumbling, toppling, and responding to forces in believable ways.

In this chapter, we will explore rigid body fundamentals, the mathematical tools required to simulate rotational motion, and practical techniques for applying forces, torques, and impulses. We'll also cover how to model real-world behaviors like inertia and discuss best practices for clean, efficient C++ implementation.

Let's begin with the foundation: what rigid bodies are and why they matter.

7.1 Introduction to Rigid Bodies

A **rigid body** is an idealized solid object that:

- Maintains a constant shape.

- Does not deform under stress.

- Moves and rotates based on applied forces and torques.

In real-world physics, no object is perfectly rigid, but for games, assuming perfect rigidity provides a good balance of realism and computational efficiency.

A rigid body in a physics engine typically maintains:

- **Position**: the location of its center of mass.

- **Orientation**: its rotation, often represented as a quaternion or rotation matrix.

- **Linear Velocity**: how fast and in what direction it's moving.

- **Angular Velocity**: how fast and around what axis it's spinning.

- **Mass** and **Inverse Mass**: governing how it responds to forces.

- **Inertia Tensor** and **Inverse Inertia Tensor**: governing how it resists rotation.

Together, these properties allow a rigid body to interact with its environment in rich, dynamic ways — rolling down hills, bouncing off surfaces, tipping over when struck, or spinning when hit off-center.

7.2 Modeling Inertia Tensors and Moments

In linear motion, mass governs how resistant an object is to changes in velocity. In rotational motion, the equivalent concept is the **moment of inertia**.

Moment of Inertia

The **moment of inertia** describes how mass is distributed relative to an axis of rotation. Intuitively:

- Objects with more mass farther from the center are harder to spin.

- Compact objects (like a sphere) are easier to rotate.

For simple shapes, moments of inertia can be calculated analytically:

Shape	Moment of Inertia
Solid Sphere	$\frac{2}{5}mr^2$
Solid Box (about center)	$\frac{1}{12}m(l^2 + w^2)$
Cylinder (about center)	$\frac{1}{2}mr^2$

Where m is mass, r is radius, and l, w are length and width.

Inertia Tensor

In 3D simulations, rotation isn't just about a single axis. Objects can rotate about any arbitrary axis, depending on how forces are applied. To handle this, we use an **inertia tensor** — a 3x3 matrix that describes how an object resists rotation around every possible axis.

The inertia tensor varies with:

- Object shape

- Mass

- Orientation (rotating the object rotates its inertia tensor)

At runtime:

- The tensor must be transformed into world space.

- The **inverse inertia tensor** is often cached for faster calculations.

Handling inertia correctly ensures that, for example, a hammer spins differently when struck at the handle versus the head.

Practical Notes

- Many engines simplify inertia for performance, approximating complex shapes with spheres, boxes, or capsules.

- If an object is static (non-movable), its inverse inertia is treated as zero, preventing any rotation.

By carefully modeling inertia, we create physical objects that feel "right" when interacting — heavy things roll slowly, lightweight things spin freely, and collisions produce satisfying motion.

7.3 Applying Forces, Torques, and Impulses

To move a rigid body in simulation, you don't just teleport it around. You apply **forces** and **torques** that cause natural motion.

Applying Linear Forces

Forces affect **linear velocity**:

$$F=ma \Rightarrow a=Fm\mathbf{F} = m\mathbf{a} \quad \Rightarrow \quad \mathbf{a} = \frac{\mathbf{F}}{m}F=ma \Rightarrow a=mF$$

Accumulating forces each frame and then integrating them produces realistic movement.

Example:

cpp

CopyEdit

```cpp
void RigidBody::applyForce(const Vector3& force) {

    accumulatedForces += force;
```

```
}
```

Applying Torques

If a force is applied at a point other than the center of mass, it generates a **torque**:

$\tau = r \times F$ \mathbf{\tau} = \mathbf{r} \times \mathbf{F} $\tau = r \times F$

Where:

- r\mathbf{r}r = vector from center of mass to point of application

- F\mathbf{F}F = force vector

Torque affects **angular acceleration**, leading to rotational motion.

Applying torque in C++:

cpp

CopyEdit

```cpp
void RigidBody::applyTorque(const Vector3& torque) {

    accumulatedTorques += torque;

}
```

Or when applying an off-center force:

cpp

CopyEdit

```cpp
void RigidBody::applyForceAtPoint(const Vector3& force,
const Vector3& point) {

    accumulatedForces += force;

    accumulatedTorques += cross(point - centerOfMass,
force);

}
```

Applying Impulses

As discussed in the previous chapter, **impulses** are instantaneous changes in velocity or angular velocity.

Impulse application for rotation:

cpp

CopyEdit

```cpp
body.angularVelocity += inverseInertiaTensorWorld *
cross(contactPoint - centerOfMass, impulse);
```

Correctly applying impulses allows for bouncing, rebounding, spinning, and other high-energy interactions without numerical instability.

7.4 Handling Rotational Motion and Angular Velocity

Just as forces change linear motion, torques change rotational motion.

The angular analog of Newton's second law:

$$\tau = I\alpha \Rightarrow \alpha = I^{-1}\tau \quad \mathbf{\tau} = I\mathbf{\alpha} \quad \Rightarrow \quad \mathbf{\alpha} = I^{-1}\mathbf{\tau} \tau = I\alpha \Rightarrow \alpha = I^{-1}\tau$$

Where:

- τ \mathbf{\tau} τ = torque

- I I = inertia tensor

- α \mathbf{\alpha} α = angular acceleration

Integrating Angular Motion

During each physics step:

1. Compute angular acceleration based on accumulated torques.

2. Update angular velocity.

3. Update orientation based on angular velocity.

In code:

cpp

CopyEdit

```
// 1. Angular acceleration

Vector3 angularAcceleration = inverseInertiaTensorWorld *
accumulatedTorques;

// 2. Angular velocity

angularVelocity += angularAcceleration * deltaTime;

// 3. Orientation update

Quaternion spin = Quaternion(0, angularVelocity.x,
angularVelocity.y, angularVelocity.z) * orientation * 0.5f;

orientation += spin * deltaTime;

orientation = normalize(orientation);
```

Note:

- The orientation must be normalized regularly to prevent drift.

- Using quaternions for rotation avoids gimbal lock and preserves stability.

Rotating the Inertia Tensor

As the object rotates, its local inertia tensor must be transformed into world space:

$$I_{world} = R I_{local} R^T$$ Iworld=RIlocalRT

Where RRR is the rotation matrix derived from the object's orientation.

Failing to update the inertia tensor correctly leads to odd, unrealistic rotational behavior.

7.5 Practical Implementation Tips

Handling rigid body dynamics in real-time C++ requires balancing **correctness**, **performance**, and **stability**.

Here are some practical guidelines:

Accumulate Forces and Torques

- Apply forces/torques throughout the frame.

- Accumulate them.

- Clear accumulators after each integration step.

This approach ensures consistent behavior regardless of the order of force applications.

Use Inverse Mass and Inverse Inertia

- Store inverse mass and inverse inertia tensor.

- Multiplying is faster and more stable than dividing by mass at runtime.

- Static objects (infinite mass) have inverse mass = 0.

Stabilize Small Rotations

- Clamp or dampen very small angular velocities.

- Prevent micro-spins from accumulating due to floating-point inaccuracies.

Normalize Orientations

- After updating quaternion orientation, normalize it.

- Prevents slow drift and breakdown of rotational stability.

Example:

cpp

CopyEdit

```cpp
orientation = normalize(orientation);
```

Separate Static and Dynamic Bodies

- Static objects (mass = infinity) don't need to update position or orientation.

- Optimize simulation by skipping unnecessary calculations for static or sleeping objects.

Manage Sleep States

- If a body's velocity and angular velocity fall below a small threshold, mark it as sleeping.

- Sleeping bodies aren't updated until an external force or collision wakes them up.

This dramatically improves performance in large, mostly-static scenes.

Rigid body dynamics bring the richness of the real world into your virtual simulations. Correctly handling forces, torques, inertia, and motion integration makes objects feel tangible, weighty, and alive.

By following the practical techniques discussed here — and carefully structuring your C++ code to handle dynamics efficiently — you are now equipped to simulate compelling physical interactions in your games and projects.

Part III: Advanced Simulation Techniques

With a solid understanding of rigid body dynamics and collision systems, it's time to explore the more sophisticated and expressive side of physics simulation. Part III focuses on the techniques that go beyond simple solid-body interactions — the simulations that bring worlds to life with soft bodies, flowing fluids, and interconnected systems.

Advanced simulation techniques allow for richer gameplay, deeper immersion, and more creative possibilities. Whether it's a flag fluttering in the wind, a character swinging on a rope, water splashing against a shoreline, or a pile of debris reacting dynamically to an explosion, these systems add realism and excitement that rigid bodies alone cannot deliver.

In this section, we'll dive into soft body physics, learn how to simulate cloth and flexible materials, explore particle-based fluid simulation, and uncover how constraint solvers can model joints, ropes, and articulated mechanisms. Each topic will combine practical math, clear explanations, and real-world C++ examples you can apply directly in your own engines or games.

By mastering these techniques, you'll move from simulating hard surfaces to creating living, reactive worlds — full of energy, complexity, and believable interaction.

Let's begin with the fascinating world of soft body physics.

Chapter 8: Soft Body Physics and Cloth Simulation

Rigid bodies are excellent for simulating solid, inflexible objects like crates, vehicles, and rocks. But not everything in the real world behaves so rigidly. Fabric ripples, rubber bends, and biological tissues compress and stretch. To capture these richer, more dynamic behaviors in a simulation, we turn to **soft body physics**.

Soft bodies introduce elasticity and deformation into your worlds, making them feel more natural and responsive. While more complex than rigid body simulation, soft bodies can be efficiently modeled with the right techniques — and the results are often spectacular.

In this chapter, we'll explore the foundations of soft body simulation, focusing on **mass-spring models**, **cloth behavior**, **basic collision handling**, and **visualization techniques**. By the end, you'll have a working understanding of how to build flexible, deformable simulations that react convincingly in real time.

Let's start by exploring the most common and practical method for simulating soft bodies: the mass-spring model.

8.1 Mass-Spring Models Explained

The **mass-spring system** is one of the simplest and most intuitive ways to simulate soft bodies.

At its core:

- **Mass points** represent small, discrete portions of the object's mass.

- **Springs** connect mass points, modeling elasticity and restoring forces.

- **Forces** and **damping** are applied to simulate stretching, compression, and resistance.

This system mimics how real materials behave on a microscopic level: small parts pull and push on each other, striving to maintain a certain shape while allowing some flexibility.

Mass Points

Each mass point (or node) maintains:

- Position

- Velocity

- Mass (or inverse mass)

- Accumulated forces

They behave similarly to small rigid bodies, responding to forces like gravity and collisions.

Springs

Each spring connects two mass points and tries to maintain a **rest length** — the natural, unstretched distance between them.

The spring force is calculated using **Hooke's Law**:

Fspring=−ks(current length−rest length)d\mathbf{F}_{spring} = -k_s (\text{current length} - \text{rest length}) \mathbf{d}Fspring=−ks(current length−rest length)d

Where:

- ksk_sks = spring stiffness coefficient

- d\mathbf{d}d = normalized direction vector between points

Springs resist both **stretching** (longer than rest length) and **compression** (shorter than rest length).

Damping

Real-world materials don't oscillate forever after being stretched — they settle over time. **Damping** models this energy loss:

Fdamping=−kd(relative velocity · d)d\mathbf{F}_{damping} = -k_d (\text{relative velocity} \cdot \mathbf{d}) \mathbf{d}Fdamping=−kd(relative velocity · d)d

Where:

- kdk_dkd = damping coefficient

- d\mathbf{d}d = normalized direction vector

Damping prevents perpetual bouncing and makes soft bodies behave realistically under dynamic forces.

Mass-Spring System in Practice

At each simulation step:

1. Calculate spring forces for all springs.

2. Add forces like gravity or external inputs.

3. Integrate motion using your chosen integration method (e.g., Semi-Implicit Euler).

4. Handle collisions (basic overlap checks and corrections).

5. Update visualization based on mass point positions.

Mass-spring models offer a good balance of **simplicity**, **flexibility**, and **performance**, making them a great fit for real-time cloth, rope, and jelly-like material simulations.

8.2 Cloth Simulation: Stretching, Bending, and Shearing

One of the most visually striking uses of soft body physics is **cloth simulation** — modeling flags, clothing, sails, or curtains that ripple and react naturally to forces like gravity, wind, or movement.

Cloth is typically simulated as a **2D grid** of mass points connected by different types of springs.

Types of Springs in Cloth Simulation

To accurately capture cloth behavior, different spring connections are used:

1. **Structural Springs** (Stretching)

   o Connect immediate horizontal and vertical neighbors.

   o Resist direct stretching or compression.

2. **Shear Springs** (Shearing)

   o Connect diagonal neighbors.

   o Resist distortion that would turn squares into rhombuses.

3. **Bend Springs** (Bending)

   o Connect next-nearest horizontal and vertical neighbors.

   o Resist folding and help maintain smoothness.

Each type of spring has its own stiffness and damping values, allowing you to fine-tune how stiff or flowing the cloth appears.

Simulation Steps for Cloth

Each frame:

- Compute forces for all springs (structural, shear, bend).

- Add external forces (gravity, wind).

- Integrate motion of mass points.

- Handle collisions (e.g., with rigid bodies or world geometry).

- Enforce constraints (optional) to prevent extreme stretching.

Boundary Conditions

In many cloth simulations:

- Some points are **pinned** (fixed in space) — like the top corners of a flag attached to a pole.

- Others are free to move.

Pinning adds realism and prevents the entire cloth from drifting away under gravity.

Wind and External Forces

Wind forces can be modeled as:

Fwind=(normal · wind direction)×wind strength$\mathbf{F}_{wind} = (\text{normal} \cdot \text{wind direction}) \times \text{wind strength}$Fwind=(normal · wind direction)×wind strength

Applying wind pressure based on surface normals produces beautiful rippling effects.

8.3 Basic Soft Body Collision Handling

Handling collisions between soft bodies and their environment is more complex than rigid body collision, but it follows familiar principles.

Point vs Surface Collisions

Since soft bodies are made of discrete mass points:

- **Each mass point** is checked for collision against surfaces (planes, spheres, boxes, etc.).

- If a point penetrates a surface, it's pushed back and its velocity is adjusted.

Simple collision response for a plane:

cpp

CopyEdit

```cpp
if (point.position.y < planeHeight) {

    point.position.y = planeHeight;

    point.velocity.y = abs(point.velocity.y) * restitution;

}
```

Where:

- restitutionrestitutionrestitution controls how "bouncy" the collision is.

This method provides a good approximation for many applications. More complex systems may:

- Detect collisions between the cloth's triangles and surfaces.

- Resolve interpenetrations more smoothly.

Self-Collision

Realistic cloth can collide with itself — folds touching other folds. Handling self-collision is computationally expensive and often omitted in real-time games for performance reasons. When needed, it's usually handled with simplified approximations (e.g., checking nearby points for overlap).

Stability and Correction

Soft bodies are vulnerable to **instability**, especially when springs become overstretched or when collisions are too aggressive.

Strategies to improve stability:

- Use smaller timesteps.

- Increase damping slightly.

- Limit maximum stretch ratio for springs.

- Apply positional correction gently over multiple frames.

8.4 Visualizing Deformation in Real-Time

Visualizing soft bodies effectively is just as important as simulating them.

Rendering Techniques

For cloth:

- Mass points form vertices of a mesh.

- Springs define edges (for debugging).

- Triangles are generated between points to form the visible surface.

- Vertex normals are recalculated each frame for proper lighting.

For jelly-like bodies:

- Mass points can control the corners of deformable bounding shapes.

- Surface smoothness can be enhanced with normal interpolation and skinning.

Debugging Visualization

During development, it's extremely helpful to:

- Draw springs as lines (colored by tension or compression).

- Draw mass points as small spheres.

- Highlight collisions visually (e.g., red points when penetrating surfaces).

Debug visualizations make it much easier to spot overstretched springs, broken constraints, or unstable oscillations.

Performance Considerations

Soft body simulations are **more expensive** than rigid bodies:

- Avoid very high-resolution meshes unless necessary.

- Update physics at a lower rate than rendering if possible (e.g., simulate at 30 Hz, render at 60 Hz).

- Use simple collision proxies (bounding boxes, spheres) instead of full mesh collision when possible.

Through careful optimization, soft body simulations can run smoothly even on modest hardware — adding a huge amount of visual richness without crippling performance.

Soft body physics and cloth simulation open new creative possibilities. Whether you're animating realistic clothing, flags waving in the breeze, or gelatinous creatures wobbling under their own weight, these techniques add flexibility, beauty, and life to your virtual worlds.

In the next chapter, we'll expand further into advanced particle-based systems, exploring **fluid simulation** and how to model water, smoke, and other dynamic materials.

Let's continue.

Chapter 9: Particle Systems and Fluid Simulation

While rigid bodies and soft bodies capture the behavior of solid and flexible materials, simulating **fluids** opens an entirely different and fascinating frontier. Water splashing, smoke rising, lava flowing — these phenomena all share a common trait: they consist of large numbers of tiny particles moving together in complex, often beautiful ways.

In games and simulations, **particle systems** provide a powerful tool for representing not just fluids, but also explosions, weather effects, magic spells, and even crowds. More advanced techniques, like **Smoothed Particle Hydrodynamics (SPH)**, allow us to model fluid behavior with surprising realism and responsiveness.

In this chapter, we'll explore the fundamentals of particle systems, dive into SPH for fluid simulation, cover how fluids interact with each other and with solid objects, and discuss performance optimization strategies for handling thousands — or even millions — of particles in real time.

Let's start with the basics: what particle systems are and how they fit into simulation frameworks.

9.1 Fundamentals of Particle Systems

At their core, particle systems are collections of small, independent points ("particles") that represent complex phenomena by their collective behavior.

Each particle typically has:

- **Position**

- **Velocity**

- **Acceleration**

- **Mass**

- **Life span** (optional, for effects like smoke dissipating)

Particles are simulated individually, but their aggregate behavior creates the illusion of continuous materials or dynamic effects.

Key Characteristics of Particle Systems

- **Discrete**: Particles are distinct entities; the fluidity emerges from their numbers.

- **Lightweight**: Particles are typically simpler than rigid bodies — no rotation, no shape beyond a point or small sphere.

- **Highly Parallelizable**: Each particle can often be updated independently, making particle systems ideal for multithreading or GPU acceleration.

Basic Particle System Workflow

Each simulation step:

1. **Apply forces**: gravity, wind, user-defined forces.

2. **Update velocities and positions**: integrate over the timestep.

3. **Handle collisions**: respond to ground, obstacles, or fluid boundaries.

4. **Spawn new particles**: if necessary for continuous effects.

5. **Remove dead particles**: if using a life span system.

In simple cases — like fire or dust — particles are completely independent. For fluid simulation, however, particles must **interact** with each other, leading us into more complex territory.

9.2 Smoothed Particle Hydrodynamics (SPH) Techniques

Smoothed Particle Hydrodynamics (SPH) is a powerful technique for simulating fluids using particle systems. Rather than treating fluid as a continuous volume, SPH models it as a collection of particles, each carrying mass, velocity, and density.

The key to SPH is that each particle's properties are influenced by its neighbors, using **smoothing kernels** to interpolate values across space.

Core Concepts in SPH

Density Estimation

Each particle computes its **density** based on neighboring particles:

$\rho i = \sum j m j W(|ri{-}rj|, h) \backslash rho\_i = \backslash sum\_j m\_j W(|\backslash mathbf\{r\}\_i - \backslash mathbf\{r\}\_j|, h) \rho i = j \sum m j W(|ri{-}rj|, h)$

Where:

- ρ_i \rho_i ρ_i = density of particle $i$ii

- m_jm_j m_j = mass of neighbor $j$jj

- WWW = smoothing kernel function

- $h$hh = smoothing radius

Common smoothing kernels include the **poly6 kernel** for density estimation.

Pressure Forces

Once density is known, **pressure** can be computed using an equation of state:

$P_i = k(\rho_i - \rho_0)$P_i = k(\rho_i - \rho_0)$P_i = k(\rho_i - \rho_0)$

Where:

- P_iP_i P_i = pressure of particle $i$ii

- $k$kk = stiffness constant

- ρ_0\rho_0 ρ_0 = rest density (target density of fluid)

Pressure forces push particles apart to resist compression:

$F_{pressure} = -\sum_j m_j \left(\frac{P_i + P_j}{2 \rho_j} \right) \nabla W(|r_i - r_j|, h)$\mathbf{F}_{pressure} = -\sum_j m_j \left(\frac{P_i + P_j}{2 \rho_j} \right) \nabla W(|\mathbf{r}_i - \mathbf{r}_j|, h)$F_{pressure} = -\sum_j m_j \left(\frac{2\rho_j}{P_i + P_j} \right) \nabla W(|r_i - r_j|, h)$

This restores fluid volume and prevents clustering.

Viscosity Forces

Viscosity models the internal friction of the fluid, smoothing out velocity differences between particles:

Fviscosity=μ∑jmjvj−viρj∇2W(|ri−rj|,h)\mathbf{F}_{viscosity} = \mu \sum_j m_j \frac{\mathbf{v}_j - \mathbf{v}_i}{\rho_j} \nabla^2 W(|\mathbf{r}_i - \mathbf{r}_j|, h)Fviscosity=μj∑mjρjvj−vi∇2W(|ri−rj|,h)

Where:

- μ\muμ = dynamic viscosity coefficient

- ∇2W\nabla^2 W∇2W = Laplacian of the smoothing kernel

Viscosity prevents "clumpy" or "sticky" behavior, making water appear fluid and continuous.

External Forces

Gravity, buoyancy, and other external forces are simply added to each particle's force accumulator.

Integration

After computing all forces:

- Accelerations are derived.

- Velocities and positions are updated using standard integration methods (e.g., Semi-Implicit Euler).

9.3 Fluid-Fluid and Fluid-Solid Interactions

Fluid-Fluid Interactions

In SPH, fluid-fluid interaction is naturally handled via neighbor influence:

- Particles influence each other's density and pressure.

- This automatically models flow, turbulence, and wave-like behavior.

Advanced SPH variants (e.g., multiphase SPH) can model interactions between different types of fluids (oil and water, for instance) with appropriate boundary conditions and different material properties.

Fluid-Solid Interactions

Handling how fluid particles interact with solid surfaces is critical for realism.

Simple collision response:

- If a particle penetrates a boundary, reflect its velocity and apply friction/damping.

cpp

CopyEdit

```cpp
if (particle.position.y < surfaceHeight) {

    particle.position.y = surfaceHeight;
```

```
    particle.velocity.y *= -restitution;

}
```

Boundary particles:

- Sometimes static "boundary particles" are used to represent surfaces, allowing
  fluid particles to interact via the same SPH force calculations.

More advanced techniques:

- Enforce boundary conditions like no-slip (fluid velocity matches solid boundary
  velocity).

- Handle porous materials (fluid passes through partially).

- Create moving solid objects (boats, paddles) that affect and are affected by fluid
  particles.

Fluid-solid interaction is where SPH shines compared to grid-based methods —
allowing complex, dynamic shapes to interact with water without needing predefined
meshes.

9.4 Optimizing Particle Physics for Games

Simulating thousands of particles every frame is expensive. Careful optimization is
essential to make particle systems and fluid simulation viable in real-time games.

Neighbor Search Optimization

Finding neighboring particles is the most expensive part of SPH. Naively checking every particle against every other particle is $O(n2)O(n^2)O(n2)$ — completely impractical for large systems.

Solutions:

- **Spatial hashing**: Map particles into a 3D grid, quickly retrieving neighbors from nearby cells.

- **Uniform grids**: Divide space into regular cells for rapid lookup.

- **Adaptive grids**: Use smaller cells where particle density is higher.

Parallelization

Particles are often independent enough to allow parallel processing:

- CPU multithreading: divide particles among cores.

- GPU acceleration: massive speedups with compute shaders.

Many modern engines simulate particle systems entirely on the GPU, enabling millions of particles at interactive framerates.

LOD (Level of Detail)

For large particle systems:

- Simulate distant particles less frequently.

- Reduce neighbor search radius at distance.

- Cull particles not visible to the camera.

This prioritizes simulation resources where they matter most for gameplay and visuals.

Stable Timestep

Fluids are sensitive to timestep size:

- Larger steps cause instability (particles explode outward).

- Smaller steps increase CPU/GPU load.

Solutions:

- Fix timestep (e.g., always 1/60s).

- Sub-step the simulation (multiple small steps per frame) if needed during intense action.

A stable timestep is often the difference between beautiful flowing water and chaotic particle chaos.

Particle systems and fluid simulation bring movement, complexity, and life into games in ways rigid bodies never could. Whether it's roaring waterfalls, rolling fog, or the subtle splash of footsteps in a puddle, these techniques add richness and dynamism that players feel intuitively.

By mastering particle fundamentals, SPH techniques, and real-time optimization strategies, you can create fluid simulations that are both breathtaking and performant — capable of running smoothly in even the most demanding interactive environments.

In the next chapter, we'll continue building deeper simulation systems — diving into **constraints, joints, and connected physical systems**.

Chapter 10: Constraint Solvers and Joints

Physical simulations often involve not just individual objects moving freely, but objects connected together in ways that restrict their motion. A door swings around a hinge. A car wheel rotates but stays fixed to the chassis. A rope pulls two characters together without letting them drift apart infinitely.

In physics engines, these kinds of relationships are handled through **constraints** and **joints**. Constraints enforce limits or conditions between bodies, shaping how they can move relative to each other. Without constraints, simulating complex machines, articulated characters, or simple swinging bridges would be nearly impossible.

In this chapter, we'll dive into how constraints are modeled and solved, how to implement common types like fixed joints, springs, and ropes, and how to combine them into sophisticated mechanisms such as ragdoll physics for dynamic character animation.

Understanding constraints opens up a powerful new layer of realism and creativity for your simulations.

10.1 Introduction to Constraints in Physics Engines

A **constraint** is a rule that restricts the relative motion of two (or more) bodies.

Constraints can:

- Limit translation (e.g., fixing two objects at a distance).

- Limit rotation (e.g., a hinge joint allows rotation around one axis only).

- Enforce complete attachment (e.g., welding two objects together).

Rather than applying forces manually every frame to enforce these restrictions, physics engines formulate constraints as mathematical conditions — often expressed as **equations** — that must be satisfied during the simulation step.

Common Examples of Constraints

- **Fixed Constraint**: Keeps two bodies locked together rigidly.

- **Hinge Constraint**: Allows rotation around a single axis (e.g., a door).

- **Slider Constraint**: Allows translation along one axis (e.g., drawer motion).

- **Spring Constraint**: Allows flexible connection with restoring forces (e.g., rope or spring).

Constraints are typically **solved** as part of the velocity update, ensuring that after forces and impulses are applied, the final velocities satisfy the constraints as closely as possible.

10.2 Implementing Fixed Joints, Springs, and Ropes

Let's look at how to implement three of the most common types of constraints: fixed joints, springs, and ropes.

Fixed Joints

A **fixed joint** completely locks two bodies together, maintaining:

- A fixed relative position

- A fixed relative orientation

To implement a fixed joint:

1. Store the initial offset between the two bodies' frames of reference.

2. During simulation:

   o Apply impulses to correct for any drift in position and orientation.

   o Solve for both linear and angular constraints.

This usually requires setting up six constraint equations (three for translation, three for rotation).

Fixed joints are useful for welding components together — for instance, attaching a character's helmet rigidly to their head.

Spring Joints

A **spring joint** connects two points with a force that:

- Pulls them back toward a desired rest distance.

- Allows some flexibility and oscillation.

Force applied by a spring follows **Hooke's Law**:

Fspring=−ks(d−drest)n\mathbf{F}_{spring} = -k_s (d - d_{rest})
\mathbf{n}Fspring=−ks(d−drest)n

Where:

- ddd = current distance

- drestd_{rest}drest = rest length

- n\mathbf{n}n = normalized vector from one point to the other

- ksk_sks = spring stiffness constant

In addition, damping is often added to prevent endless oscillation:

Fdamping=−kd(vrelative · n)n\mathbf{F}_{damping} = -k_d (\mathbf{v}_{relative}
\cdot \mathbf{n}) \mathbf{n}Fdamping=−kd(vrelative · n)n

Spring joints can model:

- Soft rope or elastic bands

- Flexible body parts

- Tensioned cables

Rope Constraints

A **rope constraint** is a special case of a spring with a hard limit:

- It allows slack (no force when loose).

- It enforces a maximum length when taut.

Implementation approach:

- If the distance between two points exceeds the rope length, apply a corrective impulse along the line connecting them.

- Otherwise, do nothing (let the points drift freely).

This simple system is highly effective for modeling swinging ropes, grappling hooks, or towing lines.

Pseudocode for rope constraint:

cpp

CopyEdit

```cpp
Vector3 delta = bodyB.position - bodyA.position;

float distance = length(delta);

if (distance > maxRopeLength) {

    Vector3 correctionDir = normalize(delta);

    float correctionMagnitude = (distance - maxRopeLength);

    Vector3 impulse = correctionDir * (correctionMagnitude
/ (bodyA.inverseMass + bodyB.inverseMass));
```

```
bodyA.position += impulse * bodyA.inverseMass;

bodyB.position -= impulse * bodyB.inverseMass;
}
```

Simple, fast, and very satisfying when tuned correctly.

10.3 Constraint Resolution Methods (Sequential Impulse, Baumgarte Stabilization)

Solving constraints efficiently and stably is one of the hardest challenges in physics engines. Let's look at two of the most practical and widely used techniques.

Sequential Impulse Solver

Instead of solving all constraints perfectly in one massive system (which would be slow and memory-heavy), most real-time physics engines use a **sequential impulse** approach:

- Iterate through each constraint.

- Apply impulses to correct velocities locally.

- Repeat for several iterations to converge toward satisfying all constraints.

The core idea is simple:

- Solve one constraint at a time.

- Update the velocities immediately.

- Let later constraints see the updated velocities.

This approach is:

- Fast and simple

- Highly parallelizable

- Good enough for real-time simulation even if it doesn't produce mathematically perfect solutions

Sequential impulse is at the heart of engines like **Box2D** and **Bullet Physics**.

Baumgarte Stabilization

Baumgarte stabilization is a technique for **correcting positional errors** over time during velocity solving.

Idea:

- Treat positional errors (e.g., slight penetrations or joint drift) as **additional velocity corrections**.

Constraint velocity target is modified to include a correction term:

107

vtarget=vdesired+βpositional_errorΔtv_{target} = v_{desired} + \beta \frac{positional_error}{\Delta t}vtarget=vdesired+βΔtpositional_error

Where:

- β\beta$\beta$ = stabilization factor (usually around 0.1 to 0.2)

- Δt\Delta tΔt = timestep

This correction slowly nudges objects back into proper constraint alignment without drastic, disruptive jumps.

Using Baumgarte stabilization:

- Avoids "jittery" corrections.

- Helps maintain joint integrity over long simulations.

Practical Tips for Solving Constraints

- **Iterate multiple times**: 10–20 iterations are typical for good convergence.

- **Warm-starting**: Use impulses from the previous frame as an initial guess to accelerate convergence.

- **Prioritize critical constraints**: Solve important joints (like character limbs) earlier in the sequence.

Efficient constraint solving is a major factor in keeping simulations stable and believable under load.

108

10.4 Building Complex Mechanisms (e.g., Ragdoll Physics)

By combining multiple joints and constraints, you can simulate **complex articulated systems** that move and react with striking realism.

Ragdoll Physics

A **ragdoll** is a collection of rigid bodies (limbs) connected by joints, forming a flexible skeletal structure that can collapse, flop, and tumble dynamically.

Typical structure:

- Bones: Upper arm, forearm, thigh, shin, spine, etc. (each a rigid body)

- Joints: Shoulder, elbow, hip, knee, neck, etc. (each a constraint)

- Constraints limit relative angles, simulating anatomical ranges of motion.

Common joints in ragdolls:

- **Cone twist constraints**: Allow rotation within a conical range (e.g., shoulders).

- **Hinge constraints**: Allow rotation along a single axis (e.g., elbows, knees).

Ragdolls must be tuned carefully to:

- Avoid unnatural twisting or locking.

- Prevent explosions due to overly tight constraints.

- Maintain stability during fast motion or collisions.

Building Other Mechanisms

Constraints also allow you to build:

- **Vehicles**: Chassis with wheel suspension joints.

- **Bridges**: Planks linked by hinge or distance constraints.

- **Puppets and Robots**: Fully articulated characters with joint motors.

- **Dynamic environments**: Chains, pendulums, swinging doors.

With constraints, you're limited only by your creativity — virtually any mechanical or biological structure can be simulated.

Constraints and joints add a new dimension of dynamism and complexity to your simulations. By mastering constraint modeling, solving, and assembly, you can build worlds full of interactivity — where machines function, characters stumble and recover, and environments react believably to player actions.

Part IV: Building Your Own Physics Engine

Up to this point, we have explored the essential pieces of real-time physics simulation — from motion and collisions to soft bodies, fluids, and constraints. Now, it's time to bring everything together into a cohesive, working system.

Part IV is dedicated to the architecture, implementation, and integration of a complete physics engine. Rather than just isolated examples, you'll learn how to design a simulation loop that manages hundreds or even thousands of objects efficiently and reliably. We'll break down the internal structure of a physics engine into clear components — bodies, solvers, collision managers, integrators — and show how they interact seamlessly to drive a dynamic, responsive virtual world.

Building your own physics engine, even a lightweight one, gives you unparalleled control over your simulation's behavior, performance, and flexibility. It also deepens your understanding of the hidden machinery inside popular engines — allowing you to extend, optimize, or even replace built-in systems when your project demands it.

By the end of this part, you will not only understand how real-time physics engines are structured but will have the knowledge to start constructing your own — tailored to your games, experiments, or creative projects.

Let's begin by looking at how a physics engine is organized under the hood.

Chapter 11: Physics Engine Architecture

A physics engine is not a single algorithm or a monolithic block of code. It's a carefully coordinated system — a living framework where different components handle motion, collisions, constraints, and responses, all synchronized to deliver a believable simulation in real time.

Whether lightweight or full-featured, all physics engines share a core structure. Understanding this architecture is crucial if you want to build your own engine from scratch or customize one for your specific needs.

In this chapter, we'll break down the high-level structure of a physics engine, explore the essential components and their responsibilities, walk through a typical update loop, and discuss how modern games benefit from modular, component-based physics systems.

By the end, you'll see clearly how all the moving parts come together — and how you can assemble them into a coherent, performant, and flexible simulation framework.

11.1 High-Level Overview of a Physics Engine

At a high level, a physics engine must answer three fundamental questions every frame:

- **Where should everything move based on the current forces?**

- **Did anything collide?**

- **How should we resolve those collisions and constraints?**

To do this, most engines follow a general three-phase process:

1. **Force Integration**:

   o Update object velocities and positions based on applied forces (gravity, user forces, etc.).

2. **Collision Detection**:

   o Broad phase: quickly find potential collisions.

   o Narrow phase: precisely determine actual collisions.

3. **Constraint Solving and Response**:

   o Resolve contacts, correct penetrations, apply friction and restitution, enforce joints and constraints.

Each phase feeds into the next, forming a complete simulation step. This cycle repeats every frame, keeping the world dynamic and reactive.

Good physics engine architecture is about maintaining this flow while allowing flexibility, scalability, and stability — especially as object counts grow or as simulations become more complex.

11.2 Core Components: World, Solvers, Colliders, Integrators

Let's dig into the major components that form a complete physics engine.

World

The **World** object is the container and manager for the entire simulation. It:

- Holds all physical bodies (rigid, soft, or particles).

- Manages global properties (gravity, timestep settings).

- Coordinates the update sequence.

In code, the World might look something like:

cpp

CopyEdit

```
class PhysicsWorld {

public:

    std::vector<RigidBody*> bodies;

    CollisionManager collisionManager;

    Solver constraintSolver;

    Vector3 gravity;
```

```
    void step(float deltaTime);

};
```

The World acts as the "brain" that calls into solvers, collision detectors, and integrators at the right time each frame.

Bodies

Each **Body** represents a physical object with:

- Position and orientation

- Velocity and angular velocity

- Mass and inertia

- Collision shape (optional)

- Forces and torques applied

Bodies can be dynamic (moving), static (immovable), or kinematic (controlled by code, but affecting others).

Rigid bodies, soft bodies, and particles are all types of bodies managed within the world.

Colliders

Colliders define the shape of objects for the purpose of collision detection.

Common collider types:

115

- Sphere

- Capsule

- Box (AABB or OBB)

- Convex hull

- Compound shapes (made of multiple primitives)

Each body can have a collider attached, defining how it participates in collision queries.

Some systems separate colliders from bodies for modularity, allowing you to swap collision shapes dynamically if needed.

Solvers

Solvers handle the complex task of enforcing physical laws:

- Resolve collision contacts (separating overlapping bodies).

- Apply impulses to simulate bounce and friction.

- Enforce constraints like joints and springs.

In a real engine, solvers are often highly optimized, with special handling for:

- Contact resolution

- Constraint systems (e.g., sequential impulse solvers)

Good solvers prioritize **stability** and **performance**, even at the cost of minor physical inaccuracies.

Integrators

Integrators advance the simulation by updating body states based on forces.

An integrator applies:

- Force accumulation → Acceleration

- Velocity updates

- Position updates

Integrators vary based on numerical methods used (e.g., Semi-Implicit Euler, Runge-Kutta). Each has trade-offs between simplicity, stability, and accuracy.

Choosing or implementing an effective integrator is key to keeping the entire system stable, especially when handling collisions and stacking objects.

11.3 Update Loop: Simulation Step by Step

A physics engine's **update loop** typically follows a consistent sequence every frame:

1. Apply Global Forces

- Apply forces like gravity to all dynamic bodies.

- Allow external systems (player input, AI) to add additional forces.

2. Integrate Velocities

- Based on accumulated forces, compute new linear and angular velocities.

cpp

CopyEdit

```cpp
body.velocity += (body.forces * body.inverseMass + gravity)
* deltaTime;

body.angularVelocity += (body.torques *
body.inverseInertiaTensor) * deltaTime;
```

3. Broad Phase Collision Detection

- Quickly generate a list of potential overlapping body pairs.

- Use AABBs, spatial partitioning, or sweep-and-prune algorithms.

4. Narrow Phase Collision Detection

- Precisely test collision for each pair.

- Generate contact points (position, normal, penetration depth).

5. Solve Constraints

- Resolve collision contacts with impulses.

- Solve all additional constraints (joints, springs).

- Apply friction and restitution effects.

Multiple solver iterations improve stability and realism.

6. Integrate Positions

- Update body positions and orientations based on corrected velocities.

cpp

CopyEdit

```cpp
body.position += body.velocity * deltaTime;

body.orientation += 0.5f * Quaternion(0,
body.angularVelocity) * body.orientation * deltaTime;

body.orientation.normalize();
```

7. Cleanup

- Clear force and torque accumulators for the next frame.

- Optionally, perform sleeping optimizations for very slow bodies.

This structure ensures that motion, collisions, and responses are processed in a clear, efficient pipeline each frame.

11.4 Component-Based Physics Systems for Games

Modern game engines often organize physics using a **component-based architecture**. Rather than rigidly tying physics behaviors to object types, each physical behavior is treated as a reusable, attachable **component**.

Typical Physics Components

- **RigidBodyComponent**: Adds physical behavior (mass, velocity, collisions) to an object.

- **ColliderComponent**: Defines the shape used for collision detection.

- **ConstraintComponent**: Connects one object to another with rules (hinges, springs, ropes).

Example:

cpp

CopyEdit

```
class GameObject {

public:

    TransformComponent transform;
```

```
RigidBodyComponent* rigidBody;

ColliderComponent* collider;

ConstraintComponent* constraint;
};
```

This flexible approach enables:

- Easily attaching or detaching physics behavior at runtime.

- Creating hybrid objects (e.g., a car with rigid body and suspension constraints).

- Managing complex scenes (e.g., hundreds of interactable objects) without rigid inheritance chains.

Advantages of Component-Based Design

- **Modularity**: Physics behaviors can be added to any object.

- **Reusability**: Systems like collision detection or solvers don't care about object types.

- **Scalability**: New physics features can be added without rewriting core object classes.

- **Decoupling**: Physics logic is cleanly separated from rendering, AI, and gameplay code.

In most modern engines — from Unity to Unreal — physics exists as a component system, and following this pattern makes your custom physics engine easier to maintain, expand, and integrate.

A well-structured physics engine is the invisible backbone of realistic gameplay. It brings consistency, responsiveness, and depth to virtual worlds, enabling players to interact with objects in ways that feel natural and intuitive.

By understanding how engines organize their worlds, manage bodies and collisions, solve constraints, and update object states, you are now equipped to start building your own custom physics engine — one tailored precisely to your game's needs and ambitions.

Chapter 12: Step-by-Step Physics Engine Construction

Designing a physics engine can seem overwhelming at first glance. However, when broken down into manageable steps, it becomes a clear and logical process — assembling familiar components one piece at a time into a fully working system.

In this chapter, we'll walk through building a simple but robust physics engine. We'll start by defining the essential data structures for rigid bodies, move into force management, set up the collision detection pipeline, handle contact resolution, and finally, expand the system to support soft bodies and particle-based simulations.

By the end, you'll have a roadmap to guide the construction of your own physics engine — whether for a specific game project or for mastering the art of real-time physical simulation.

Let's start with the foundation: creating rigid body classes.

12.1 Creating Rigid Body Classes

The rigid body is the fundamental unit of any physics simulation. It represents an object that can move and rotate based on physical forces.

A minimal **RigidBody** class includes:

cpp

CopyEdit

```
class RigidBody {
```

```cpp
public:

    Vector3 position;

    Quaternion orientation;

    Vector3 velocity;

    Vector3 angularVelocity;


    float mass;

    float inverseMass;

    Matrix3x3 inertiaTensor;

    Matrix3x3 inverseInertiaTensor;


    Vector3 accumulatedForces;

    Vector3 accumulatedTorques;


    bool isStatic;


    RigidBody(float mass);
```

```
void applyForce(const Vector3& force);

void applyTorque(const Vector3& torque);

void integrate(float deltaTime);
```
};

Important Design Notes:

- **Inverse mass** and **inverse inertia** are precomputed for efficiency.

- Static bodies (immovable) have `inverseMass = 0.0f`.

- Forces and torques are **accumulated** during the frame before integration.

- Rigid bodies handle both **linear** and **angular** motion.

By separating data and behavior cleanly, the RigidBody class stays flexible for both simple and complex simulations.

12.2 Implementing Force Accumulators

Managing forces is crucial. Instead of applying changes immediately when a force is added, we **accumulate** forces throughout the frame and integrate them all at once during the update step.

This ensures that multiple forces from different sources (gravity, collisions, user input) combine correctly.

Applying Forces

cpp

CopyEdit

```cpp
void RigidBody::applyForce(const Vector3& force) {

    accumulatedForces += force;

}
```

Applying a torque works similarly:

cpp

CopyEdit

```cpp
void RigidBody::applyTorque(const Vector3& torque) {

    accumulatedTorques += torque;

}
```

Applying a force at a point generates both a force and a torque:

cpp

CopyEdit

```cpp
void RigidBody::applyForceAtPoint(const Vector3& force,
const Vector3& point) {

    accumulatedForces += force;

    accumulatedTorques += cross(point - position, force);
```

}

Integration Step

During the physics step, the integration looks like this:

cpp

CopyEdit

```cpp
void RigidBody::integrate(float deltaTime) {

    if (inverseMass == 0.0f) return; // Static body

    // Linear motion

    Vector3 acceleration = accumulatedForces * inverseMass;

    velocity += acceleration * deltaTime;

    position += velocity * deltaTime;

    // Angular motion

    Vector3 angularAcceleration = inverseInertiaTensor *
accumulatedTorques;

    angularVelocity += angularAcceleration * deltaTime;


    Quaternion spin(0, angularVelocity.x,
angularVelocity.y, angularVelocity.z);
```

```
    orientation += spin * orientation * 0.5f * deltaTime;

    orientation.normalize();

    // Clear accumulators

    accumulatedForces = Vector3(0, 0, 0);

    accumulatedTorques = Vector3(0, 0, 0);

}
```

This setup ensures all forces are considered before motion is updated, keeping the system stable and responsive.

12.3 Collision Detection Pipeline

Now that objects can move, we need to detect and respond to collisions. This requires a two-phase **collision detection pipeline**.

Broad Phase

First, quickly eliminate pairs of bodies that are too far apart to collide:

- AABB overlap checks

- Spatial partitioning (grids, trees)

Broad phase output: a list of candidate body pairs.

Narrow Phase

128

For each candidate pair:

- Perform precise collision tests based on shapes (spheres, boxes, capsules).

- Generate **contact points**, including:

  - Contact position

  - Collision normal

  - Penetration depth

Example sphere-sphere collision test:

cpp

CopyEdit

```cpp
bool sphereSphereCollision(const Sphere& a, const Sphere&
b, Contact& contact) {

    Vector3 delta = b.center - a.center;

    float distSq = delta.lengthSquared();

    float radiusSum = a.radius + b.radius;


    if (distSq > radiusSum * radiusSum) return false;
```

```
    float distance = sqrt(distSq);

    contact.normal = distance > 0 ? delta / distance :
Vector3(1, 0, 0);

    contact.point = a.center + contact.normal * a.radius;

    contact.penetration = radiusSum - distance;

    return true;

}
```

Efficient narrow phase collision detection ensures only real collisions proceed to response handling.

12.4 Contact Manifolds and Response Systems

Once a collision is detected, we need to resolve it so objects don't remain overlapped or pass through each other.

Contact Manifolds

A **contact manifold** stores one or more contact points between two bodies during a collision.

Each contact contains:

- World position of contact

- Collision normal

- Penetration depth

- Relative velocity

Manifolds improve stability by:

- Storing multiple contacts per collision (especially important for flat surfaces).

- Allowing better impulse distribution across large contact patches.

Impulse-Based Collision Response

For each contact:

1. Compute relative velocity.

2. Compute impulse needed to separate bodies.

3. Apply the impulse to both bodies.

Impulse calculation:

cpp

```
float velocityAlongNormal = dot(relativeVelocity,
contact.normal);

if (velocityAlongNormal > 0) return; // Separating


float e = min(bodyA.restitution, bodyB.restitution);

float j = -(1 + e) * velocityAlongNormal;

j /= bodyA.inverseMass + bodyB.inverseMass;


Vector3 impulse = j * contact.normal;

bodyA.velocity -= impulse * bodyA.inverseMass;

bodyB.velocity += impulse * bodyB.inverseMass;
```

Positional Correction

To fix penetration:

132

cpp

CopyEdit

```cpp
const float percent = 0.8f;

const float slop = 0.01f;

float correctionMagnitude = max(contact.penetration - slop,
0.0f) / (bodyA.inverseMass + bodyB.inverseMass);

Vector3 correction = correctionMagnitude * percent *
contact.normal;

bodyA.position -= correction * bodyA.inverseMass;

bodyB.position += correction * bodyB.inverseMass;
```

Combining impulses and positional correction gives smooth, responsive collision handling.

12.5 Integrating Soft Bodies and Particle Systems

Once rigid body dynamics are working, adding soft bodies and particle systems becomes a matter of extending your simulation loop carefully.

Soft Body Extension

Soft bodies use:

- Mass points (like tiny rigid bodies).

- Springs connecting mass points (applying forces).

At each frame:

1. Update spring forces.

2. Apply gravity and external forces.

3. Integrate motion for each point.

4. Handle collisions individually per point.

Soft bodies often have their own specialized collision response — simpler but less strict than rigid bodies.

Particle System Extension

Particles are simpler still:

- No rotation, no inertia tensor.

- Often affected only by external forces (e.g., gravity, wind).

Each frame:

- Apply forces.

- Integrate velocity and position.

- Cull dead particles if necessary.

Particles can also participate in broad phase spatial partitioning, allowing efficient neighbor searches for effects like fluid simulation.

By building up these systems — rigid bodies, force management, collision detection, contact resolution, and extensible support for soft bodies and particles — you create a real, functional physics engine.

From this foundation, you can continue to add more advanced features: constraints, joints, sleeping systems for performance, GPU acceleration for particle systems, and highly optimized solvers for large-scale environments.

Chapter 13: Integrating the Physics Engine with a Simple Game

Building a physics engine is a major achievement, but real magic happens when you bring it to life inside an actual game environment. Watching objects move, collide, and react dynamically creates a sense of realism and interactivity that static worlds can never match.

In this chapter, we'll walk through integrating your physics engine into a simple project — starting with a 2D sandbox of bouncing balls, expanding to a 3D box stacking simulation, rendering debug visualizations to better understand physical behavior, and covering common mistakes to avoid during integration.

This practical experience ties everything together — from forces and collisions to rendering and game loop synchronization — giving you a full understanding of how physics and gameplay work hand-in-hand.

Let's start by setting up our first simple physics-driven game world.

13.1 Setting Up a 2D Sandbox (Bouncing Balls)

The easiest way to test your physics engine is to create a **2D sandbox** where basic objects move and collide.

Step 1: Create Simple Rigid Bodies

Use your existing RigidBody class, but constrain movement to the X and Y axes only. Ignore Z entirely or fix Z = 0.

Each ball will have:

- Position (2D)

- Velocity (2D)

- Radius (for collision detection)

Gravity acts downward (negative Y).

Step 2: Handle World Boundaries

To prevent balls from falling forever or leaving the screen:

- Add static "walls" (top, bottom, left, right).

- Or implement simple boundary checks:

cpp

CopyEdit

```cpp
if (position.x - radius < 0) {

    position.x = radius;

    velocity.x *= -restitution;

}

if (position.x + radius > screenWidth) {
```

```
    position.x = screenWidth - radius;

    velocity.x *= -restitution;

}

if (position.y - radius < 0) {

    position.y = radius;

    velocity.y *= -restitution;

}
```

Step 3: Add Ball-Ball Collisions

Use circle-circle collision detection:

- If two balls are overlapping, resolve their velocities using impulse-based response.

- Correct their positions slightly to eliminate penetration.

Step 4: Launch and Observe

Spawn a few dozen balls with random positions, velocities, and sizes. Let them bounce and collide naturally under gravity.

You now have a fully functioning, visually impressive 2D physics sandbox — perfect for testing force application, collision response, and stability under many interacting objects.

13.2 Expanding to 3D (Simple Box Stacking Simulation)

After validating your engine in 2D, the next step is to move into full **3D simulation**.

One of the best initial 3D tests is **box stacking**:

- Stack multiple rigid bodies (boxes) vertically.

- Observe how they balance, tip over, and collapse under gravity and collisions.

Step 1: Create 3D Rigid Bodies

Ensure your RigidBody class supports:

- 3D position and orientation (using quaternions).

- 3D velocities and angular velocities.

- 3D inertia tensors.

Step 2: Implement Box Colliders

Use Axis-Aligned Bounding Boxes (AABBs) or simple oriented boxes for collision detection.

Broad phase:

- Use AABB overlap tests for initial filtering.

Narrow phase:

- Apply box-box collision detection.

- Resolve with contact manifolds and impulses.

Step 3: Arrange Boxes

Spawn several boxes:

- Align them in vertical stacks or grids.

- Apply random perturbations to starting velocities or rotations.

Step 4: Gravity and Friction

Make sure:

- Gravity is applied downward along the Y-axis.

- Friction is enabled in collision response to allow realistic sliding and resting.

Step 5: Observe Stability

Watch how boxes:

- Bounce slightly on impact.

- Settle naturally into stable resting configurations.

- Topple realistically if pushed off-balance.

This simulation validates:

- Correct mass and inertia handling.

- Stable integration under multiple contact points.

- Robustness of collision and contact resolution systems.

13.3 Rendering Physics Data (Debug Draws and Visualizers)

Understanding what's happening inside the physics simulation often requires more than just watching objects move — especially when debugging subtle issues like tunneling, jitter, or incorrect collision normals.

Adding a **debug visualization system** helps tremendously.

Common Debug Draws

- **Collision Shapes**:

  o Draw spheres, boxes, or hulls used for collision detection.

- **Contact Points**:

  - Draw small markers (dots or crosses) where collisions occur.

- **Collision Normals**:

  - Draw arrows from contact points showing collision normal directions.

- **Velocity Vectors**:

  - Draw lines showing current object velocities.

Example simple draw call:

cpp

CopyEdit

```
drawLine(contactPoint, contactPoint + normal * 0.5f,
Color::Red);
```

Integration with Render Loop

In your rendering system:

- After rendering the normal scene, switch to wireframe mode.

- Draw all physics debug primitives on top of the scene.

- Use different colors for different features (e.g., green for bounding volumes, red for contact points).

Benefits

- Quickly spot overlapping colliders.

- Visualize where impulses are being applied.

- Understand how constraints and joints behave over time.

- Diagnose tunneling or stability problems.

Debug draws are an essential tool for any physics engine developer — and they also look very cool when turned into gameplay features (e.g., physics visualization modes).

13.4 Common Integration Pitfalls to Avoid

Integrating a physics engine into a real-time game environment presents several common challenges. Being aware of these can save you countless hours of confusion and frustration.

Mismatched Time Steps

Problem:

- Physics is simulated at a different rate than rendering, causing jitter or inconsistencies.

Solution:

- Use a **fixed timestep** for physics (e.g., always 1/60s), independent of rendering frame rate.

- Accumulate elapsed time and run multiple physics steps if needed per frame.

cpp

CopyEdit

```cpp
const float fixedDeltaTime = 1.0f / 60.0f;

float accumulator = 0.0f;


void update(float deltaTime) {

    accumulator += deltaTime;

    while (accumulator >= fixedDeltaTime) {

        physicsWorld.step(fixedDeltaTime);

        accumulator -= fixedDeltaTime;

    }

}
```

Incorrect Collision Shapes
144

Problem:

- Visual models and collision shapes are misaligned, causing "invisible walls" or "ghost collisions."

Solution:

- Always ensure collision shapes match the rendered mesh size and orientation.

- Use debug draw to verify alignment.

Overconstrained Systems

Problem:

- Applying too many conflicting constraints causes instability and jittering.

Solution:

- Design joints carefully.

- Relax constraint limits slightly if necessary (allow a small degree of flexibility).

- Prioritize critical constraints if solver iterations are limited.

Inconsistent Units

Problem:

- Mixing units (e.g., meters for physics, pixels for rendering) leads to nonsensical behavior.

Solution:

- Choose a consistent unit system:

    o 1 unit = 1 meter (common choice).

    o Adjust rendering and physics accordingly.

Excessive Penetration and Correction

Problem:

- Fast-moving objects pass through each other without detecting collisions ("tunneling").

Solution:

- Implement continuous collision detection (CCD) if needed for critical objects.

- Reduce maximum timestep size.

- Increase collision margins slightly.

Integrating your physics engine into a live game world is one of the most satisfying stages of development. It transforms abstract data into real, visible, interactive motion — a dynamic stage for gameplay to unfold.

With a 2D sandbox, a 3D stacking simulation, debug visualization, and awareness of common pitfalls, you now have all the tools to deploy your physics system confidently and creatively.

Part V: Optimization and Real-World Extensions

Building a working physics engine is a major accomplishment, but bringing it to production quality — capable of running efficiently in real-world games — requires a new level of refinement. Part V focuses on the techniques and strategies that take your engine from basic functionality to high-performance, robust simulation.

In this section, we'll dive into optimization methods for large-scale scenes, techniques for reducing computational overhead, and best practices for maintaining stability even under extreme conditions. We'll also explore real-world extensions like continuous collision detection (CCD), advanced constraint systems, and special considerations for multiplayer synchronization.

Whether you're targeting high frame rates on limited hardware, building massive interactive worlds, or ensuring consistency across networked simulations, mastering these optimizations is essential. This is where physics simulation becomes not just technically impressive but production-ready — able to meet the demands of modern games, VR experiences, and large-scale simulations.

Let's begin by exploring the key optimization techniques that keep physics engines fast, stable, and scalable.

Chapter 14: Performance Optimization Strategies

As physics engines grow more complex and simulate larger, denser worlds, maintaining performance becomes critical. Even a perfectly designed simulation can become a bottleneck if it doesn't scale efficiently across available hardware resources.

Performance optimization isn't about guessing — it's about methodically identifying real problems, applying targeted solutions, and balancing complexity with measurable gains.

In this chapter, we'll explore practical strategies for making your physics engine faster and more scalable. We'll start with profiling and bottleneck analysis, move into optimizing memory access patterns, introduce SIMD (Single Instruction Multiple Data) techniques for processing many objects simultaneously, and discuss the basics of multithreading physics simulations.

By mastering these techniques, you can ensure your engine handles hundreds — or even thousands — of objects in real time without compromising stability or gameplay responsiveness.

Let's begin where all good optimization efforts start: profiling.

14.1 Profiling and Bottleneck Analysis

Before diving into optimization, it's essential to remember one golden rule:

Don't optimize what you haven't measured.

Optimizing code without knowing where the real problems lie can easily waste time and even make performance worse.

Step 1: Profiling the Engine

Use a profiler (such as Visual Studio Profiler, VerySleepy, or built-in engine profiling tools) to gather data:

- Frame time breakdown (rendering vs physics vs other systems)

- Time spent per function or per system

- Cache misses, CPU stalls, memory access patterns

Focus specifically on:

- Collision detection phases (broad phase, narrow phase)

- Constraint solvers (contact resolution, joint solving)

- Integrators (rigid body updates)

Look for:

- Functions with the highest cumulative time

- Hotspots with unusually high call counts

- Memory bandwidth bottlenecks (lots of cache misses)

Step 2: Identifying Bottlenecks

Once profiling is complete:

- **Sort hotspots** by total frame time contribution.

- **Rank** optimization targets: prioritize slowest parts with the biggest impact first.

- **Understand** whether the problem is CPU-bound, memory-bound, or synchronization-bound.

Common bottlenecks in physics engines:

- Collision detection (especially narrow phase)

- Memory access inefficiency (scattered body data)

- Solver iterations (especially with many stacked contacts)

- Poor parallelism (physics running on only one core)

Optimization is not about fixing everything — it's about fixing the right things.

14.2 Cache-Friendly Memory Layouts

Modern CPUs are extremely fast at executing instructions — but accessing main memory is relatively slow. **Cache performance** often makes or breaks physics engine speed.

Physics simulations naturally involve:

- Iterating over lots of bodies.

- Accessing related data (positions, velocities, forces) in tight loops.

To maximize performance, **memory access must be cache-friendly**.

Structure of Arrays (SoA) vs Array of Structures (AoS)

Traditional approach (**Array of Structures**):

cpp

CopyEdit

```cpp
struct RigidBody {

    Vector3 position;

    Vector3 velocity;

    float mass;

};
```

```cpp
RigidBody bodies[1000];
```

Problem:

- Accessing position or velocity separately results in unnecessary cache loading (loads entire structs even if you need only one field).

Optimized approach (**Structure of Arrays**):

cpp

CopyEdit

```cpp
Vector3 positions[1000];

Vector3 velocities[1000];

float masses[1000];
```

Advantages:

- Tight, predictable memory access patterns.

- Preloading multiple data points in a single cache line.

- Great for SIMD processing.

For physics:

- Positions, velocities, and forces are often processed independently.

- SoA layouts allow clean separation and batch processing of similar data.

Data Locality in Collision Detection

Broad and narrow phase collision detection benefit enormously from:

- Pre-sorting bodies spatially (spatial coherence).

- Grouping colliders that are near each other in memory.

- Maintaining bounding volumes in contiguous arrays.

This minimizes cache misses and makes neighbor queries faster and more scalable.

14.3 SIMD (Single Instruction Multiple Data) Techniques

Modern CPUs support SIMD instructions — allowing a single instruction to operate on multiple pieces of data at once.

For example:

- Adding four vectors together can be done in **one** operation instead of four.

Physics simulations are naturally **data-parallel**:

- You often apply the same operations to many bodies simultaneously (gravity, integration, collision detection).

SIMD allows dramatic speedups when applied properly.

Typical SIMD Applications in Physics

- Applying gravity to all bodies:

  - Load multiple velocities at once.

  - Apply gravity vectors simultaneously.

- Vector math (dot products, cross products).

- AABB overlap tests during broad phase.

- Mass-spring force evaluations in soft bodies.

Simple SIMD Example (Pseudocode)

Traditional (scalar):

cpp

CopyEdit

```
for (int i = 0; i < numBodies; ++i) {
```

```cpp
    velocities[i].y += gravity * deltaTime;
}
```

SIMD (conceptually):

cpp

CopyEdit

```cpp
for (int i = 0; i < numBodies; i += 4) {
    velocitiesBatch = load4(velocities[i]);
    velocitiesBatch.y += gravity * deltaTime;
    store4(velocities[i], velocitiesBatch);
}
```

Using SIMD libraries like:

- SSE / AVX intrinsics (low-level, fast but complex)

- ISPC (Intel SPMD Program Compiler)

- Higher-level abstraction libraries like Eigen, glm SIMD wrappers

can make the transition to SIMD much smoother.

156

Important Note

Before applying SIMD, ensure:

- Memory is aligned properly (16-byte or 32-byte aligned arrays).

- Operations actually benefit from vectorization (small loops don't always gain much).

SIMD shines most when applied to **large batches** of similar operations.

14.4 Multithreading Physics Simulations (Basics)

Today's hardware expects developers to use multiple cores. Physics simulations can — and should — take advantage of multithreading to achieve massive speedups.

What to Parallelize?

Ideal targets for multithreading:

- **Broad phase collision detection**:

  o Each region of space can be processed independently.

- **Narrow phase collision tests**:

  o Each candidate pair can be tested in parallel.

- **Force integration**:

    ○ Each rigid body can be updated independently.

- **Constraint solving (partially)**:

    ○ Constraints that do not overlap bodies can be solved in parallel.

Basic Parallelization Strategy

- Divide the list of bodies into chunks.

- Assign chunks to different worker threads.

- Use thread-safe structures or thread-local accumulators when necessary.

Example using a simple thread pool:

cpp

CopyEdit

```cpp
parallelForEach(bodies, [](RigidBody& body) {

    body.integrate(deltaTime);

});
```

Libraries like:

- OpenMP

- C++ standard library `<thread>` and `<future>`

- Custom lightweight thread pools

can make this approach relatively easy to integrate.

Synchronization Challenges

Be cautious:

- Avoid multiple threads writing to the same memory (race conditions).

- Divide work cleanly: assign each thread a separate set of objects when possible.

- Solve overlapping constraints carefully: constraint graphs can be partitioned or solved iteratively.

Advanced Topics

For larger, more complex physics engines:

- **Task-based parallelism** (dynamic scheduling of small work units).

- **SIMD inside multithreaded loops** for ultimate performance.

- **Job systems** (like Unity's C# Job System or Unreal's Task Graph).

But even basic multithreading can easily **double or triple** performance for medium-scale simulations.

Optimization isn't a single technique — it's a mindset. By profiling smartly, laying out memory cleanly, using SIMD where appropriate, and spreading the load across multiple cores, you can dramatically boost your physics engine's performance while maintaining flexibility and robustness.

Chapter 15: Networking and Multiplayer Physics Challenges

Physics simulation in a single-player game is challenging enough. But once you move into **networked multiplayer**, the complexity grows dramatically.

In a multiplayer setting, every player's machine must share a consistent, believable version of the world — even though:

- Players have different network latencies.

- Packets can arrive late, out of order, or not at all.

- Simulations must continue to feel smooth and responsive despite these problems.

Synchronizing physics over a network without making the game feel laggy, unresponsive, or unfair is a delicate balance between authority, prediction, correction, and compensation.

In this chapter, we'll dive into the core challenges of multiplayer physics, explore solutions like client-side prediction and server reconciliation, discuss techniques for handling lag and jitter, and walk through practical examples of building physics systems that work smoothly across a network.

Let's begin by understanding the basic dynamics of networked physics.

15.1 Physics in Networked Multiplayer Games

At its heart, multiplayer physics boils down to two key facts:

- Physics simulations are **deterministic** on a given machine (given the same inputs and initial conditions, you get the same result).

- Networks are **non-deterministic** (variable delays, packet loss).

Typical Multiplayer Architecture

Most multiplayer games follow a **client-server** model:

- **Clients**: Predict and simulate locally to stay responsive.

- **Server**: Runs the authoritative physics simulation.

- Clients receive updates from the server to correct or override their local predictions.

Key Multiplayer Challenges

- **Latency**: Time delay between a client sending an input and seeing the server's authoritative result.

- **Packet Loss**: Missing updates causing temporary desynchronization.

- **Divergence**: Small differences in simulation leading to visible mismatches between client and server states.

- **Cheating**: Trusting clients too much can open the door to hacks and exploits.

These problems are especially pronounced in physics-heavy games where the precise state of moving objects determines gameplay outcomes (e.g., shooter projectiles, racing vehicles, fighting games).

Thus, careful design is needed to keep physics simulations **smooth, fair, and secure** across the network.

15.2 Client-Side Prediction and Server Reconciliation

One of the most powerful solutions to network physics problems is **client-side prediction** paired with **server reconciliation**.

Client-Side Prediction

Rather than waiting for the server to confirm every action, the client **predicts** immediate effects based on local input.

Example:

- Player presses jump.

- Client immediately simulates jump locally, updating physics.

- Server later sends authoritative confirmation.

This prediction hides latency, keeping controls responsive.

In physics:

- Players simulate their own rigid body based on inputs.

- Clients simulate collisions, forces, and constraints locally.

- Some predicted interactions with other players or objects may occur.

Prediction is critical for fast-paced, responsive multiplayer gameplay.

Server Reconciliation

Eventually, the server sends its authoritative simulation state back to the client.

If the client's prediction differs from the server's state:

- The client must **correct** its local simulation.

- Ideally, this correction is **smooth** and minimally disruptive (not teleporting players noticeably).

Basic reconciliation steps:

1. Compare local predicted state to server state.

2. If the error exceeds a threshold, adjust local state toward server truth.

3. Optionally, "rewind" and re-simulate a few frames based on corrected state.

Simple correction:

cpp

CopyEdit

```
Vector3 positionError = serverPosition -
clientPredictedPosition;

if (positionError.length() > acceptableThreshold) {

    clientPredictedPosition = serverPosition;

}
```

More advanced systems perform smooth interpolation or state blending over several frames to hide corrections visually.

15.3 Handling Lag, Jitter, and Divergence

Even with prediction and reconciliation, network imperfections cause real challenges.

Dealing with Lag

Lag is inevitable, but you can **hide** it creatively:

- **Extrapolation**: Predict movement based on last known velocity when updates are delayed.

- **Dead reckoning**: Predict position until a correction arrives.

- **Interpolation delay**: Render slightly in the past (e.g., 100ms delay) so you always have a recent server state to interpolate between.

Choosing the right approach depends on gameplay style:

- Fast twitch games (shooters) prioritize prediction.

- Slower, more tactical games may prioritize interpolation for smoothness.

Smoothing Corrections

When corrections are necessary:

- **Blend** smoothly between old and corrected state over several frames.

- Avoid harsh teleports unless the error is extreme.

Simple blending:

cpp

CopyEdit

```cpp
Vector3 newPosition = lerp(clientPosition, serverPosition,
correctionFactor * deltaTime);
```

Where `correctionFactor` is tuned based on acceptable visual latency and responsiveness.

Managing Divergence

Divergence happens when small differences in physics inputs cause large mismatches over time.

Sources of divergence:

- Floating-point inconsistencies across machines.

- Different simulation timesteps.

- Missing collision detections due to tiny variations.

Solutions:

- **Lockstep Simulation**: Ensure all players run identical physics steps based on shared inputs (common in RTS games).

- **Authoritative Server**: Server resolves collisions, contacts, and forces. Clients follow.

- **Rollback and Re-Simulate**: Roll back a few frames on divergence and reapply inputs (used heavily in fighting games).

In most action games, fully deterministic lockstep is impractical. Server authority with smart prediction and reconciliation is the dominant strategy.

15.4 Practical Examples: Physics Over a Network

Let's walk through two simple, real-world multiplayer physics examples.

Example 1: Bouncing Ball Arena

In a simple multiplayer ball game:

- Each client controls a ball.

- Balls collide with the environment and each other.

- Physics must feel responsive.

Design:

- Clients predict ball motion locally based on player input.

- Server simulates ball motion authoritatively.

- Server periodically sends ball states (position, velocity) to all clients.

- Clients reconcile if their ball drifts too far from server ball.

Collision with static environment (walls) can be predicted locally safely.
Collision between players' balls might require server authority to prevent cheating.

Example 2: Multiplayer Racing Game

In a networked racing game:

- Vehicles are highly physics-driven (mass, friction, suspension).

Design:

- Clients predict their own car's physics entirely.

- Server verifies collisions, lap times, and critical events (like ramming opponents).

- Small state corrections are blended into the car's motion to hide discrepancies.

- For visual smoothness, other players' cars are interpolated, not predicted.

Racing games balance aggressive prediction for self-controlled vehicles with graceful interpolation for opponents.

Networking physics is one of the hardest problems in real-time game development — but it's also one of the most rewarding to solve. A responsive, fair, and stable multiplayer physics simulation elevates gameplay from simply good to unforgettable.

By understanding prediction, reconciliation, divergence management, and practical design patterns, you can create multiplayer physics experiences that feel smooth, natural, and competitive across diverse network conditions.

Chapter 16: Advanced Topics and Future Directions

At this stage, you have all the essential building blocks for a capable, high-performance physics engine. But real-time physics continues to evolve, pushing into new domains — from massive destructible terrains to immersive VR interactions and hybrid systems that blur the line between simulation and animation.

In this chapter, we'll explore several advanced topics that expand the possibilities of your physics engine:

- Simulating deformable terrains,

- Building basic vehicle dynamics,

- Adapting simulations for Virtual Reality (VR),

- And integrating procedural animation with physical motion.

These topics hint at the future of real-time physics development — combining physical accuracy with creative flexibility to create more believable, engaging, and interactive worlds.

Let's begin with dynamic terrains and how they reshape traditional rigid environments.

16.1 Terrain and Deformation Physics

Most physics simulations assume static environments — ground planes, walls, floors that never change. But modern games increasingly demand **dynamic terrains** that can bend, break, deform, or even be reshaped by players.

Dynamic Terrain Types

- **Heightfield Deformation**:

    - Modify a grid of height values dynamically.

    - Example: footprints in snow, craters from explosions.

- **Voxel-Based Terrain**:

    - Represent terrain as a 3D grid of small cubes (voxels).

    - Allows full volumetric deformation (digging, tunneling).

- **Mesh Deformation**:

    - Modify vertices of a polygonal mesh at runtime.

    - Ideal for soft, elastic terrains (mud, sand).

Physical Challenges

Dynamic terrains complicate physics:

- Colliders must update as the terrain changes.

- Contact points and normals shift as ground deforms.

- Broad phase structures must adapt to changing environments.

Strategies for Handling Deformable Terrain

- **Chunked Updates**: Only update physics colliders in regions where deformation occurs.

- **Simplified Collision Proxies**: Use approximate colliders (spheres, capsules) for dynamic regions.

- **Deferred Rebuilding**: Deform visual terrain immediately, rebuild physics colliders during idle time to avoid stalling the main thread.

Example: Footprint Simulation

1. Character steps on deformable snow.

2. Deform local heightfield beneath foot.

3. Update local collider if necessary.

4. Continue simulation — next step interacts with modified terrain.

Dynamic terrains enhance immersion, allowing players to leave a physical mark on the world — a powerful addition to any simulation.

16.2 Vehicle Physics Basics

Simulating vehicles adds another layer of complexity. Vehicles involve multiple moving parts (wheels, suspension), nonlinear forces (tire friction), and strong stability requirements.

Even basic vehicle simulation demands careful modeling of key forces:

Core Forces in Vehicle Physics

- **Engine Force**: Drives wheels based on throttle input.

- **Braking Force**: Opposes motion during braking.

- **Rolling Resistance**: Opposes motion constantly (from ground contact).

- **Aerodynamic Drag**: Increases with speed.

- **Tire Friction**: Provides lateral grip for steering and cornering.

Suspension Systems

A critical part of believable vehicle behavior is suspension:

- Each wheel is connected to the chassis by a spring-damper system.

- Suspension absorbs shocks from terrain and maintains ground contact.

Simple suspension force:

$$F_{spring} = -k_s(x - x_{rest}) - k_d v$$

Where:

- k_s = spring stiffness,

- x = current spring length,

- x_{rest} = rest length,

- k_d = damping coefficient,

- v = relative velocity.

Suspension stabilizes vehicles, preventing unrealistic bouncing or tipping.

Simplified Vehicle Model (Raycast Vehicle)

Rather than simulating full 3D wheel colliders, many engines use **raycast vehicles**:

- Raycasts from chassis down to the ground detect contact points.

- Suspension forces are applied along raycast normals.

- Wheels are visual-only models animated based on physics results.

Benefits:

- Greatly reduces collision complexity.

- Easier tuning and more stable behavior.

- Sufficient for most arcade-style driving games.

Example: Basic Car Loop

Each frame:

1. Raycast wheels to detect ground.

2. Apply suspension forces.

3. Apply engine/brake forces.

4. Integrate chassis rigid body motion.

5. Animate wheel models based on physics.

Simulating even a basic car requires coordinating multiple forces, but it brings a thrilling sense of realism and control to any game.

16.3 VR Physics Considerations

Virtual Reality (VR) introduces new demands on physics engines. In VR, players expect to interact with the world **directly and physically** — grabbing objects, throwing them, climbing, or pushing them aside naturally.

VR amplifies both technical and perceptual challenges:

- **Low Latency**: Physics must run smoothly at very high frame rates (typically 90 Hz or more).

- **Precise Interaction**: Tiny simulation inaccuracies are much more noticeable when players use their real hands.

- **Responsiveness**: Physical objects must react immediately and believably to hand motions.

Challenges Specific to VR Physics

- **Hand Interactions**:

    - How do you make an object feel properly "grabbable"?

    - Objects should move naturally but also respect physical constraints.

- **Force Feedback Simulation**:

    - VR controllers can't physically resist your hand.

- Fake "forces" must be simulated by slowing down or constraining object motion when appropriate.

- **Player Strength Exaggeration**:

  - In real life, a person can't easily throw a refrigerator — but in VR, fast hand motion might cause massive forces.

  - Apply **mass-based dampening** or **motion clamping** to limit unrealistic object launches.

Best Practices for VR Physics

- **Attach grabbed objects to hands via soft constraints**:

  - A spring-damper system between the hand and the object.

  - Smoothes out jitter while allowing natural movement.

- **Use prediction and smoothing**:

  - Predict near-future hand positions for more responsive object behavior.

  - Smooth small simulation errors to avoid perceived instability.

- **Limit mass manipulation**:

  - Restrict which objects are grab-able or adjust mass dynamically during interaction.

Properly tuned, VR physics can create breathtakingly immersive experiences — giving players the true feeling of presence in a living, physical world.

16.4 Procedural Animation and Physics Integration

As physics simulations become more advanced, the boundary between **animation** and **physics** continues to blur.

Rather than predefining all object motions, modern games increasingly use **procedural animation** — dynamic movement generated at runtime — often blended with or driven by physics systems.

Examples of Physics-Animation Blending

- **Ragdoll Recovery:**

  - After a physics-driven fall, characters blend smoothly back into walking or idle animations.

- **Dynamic Cloth and Hair:**

  - Character clothing, capes, and hair are driven partly by physics but constrained to animated bones.

- **Locomotion Adaptation:**

  - Characters adjust foot placement based on terrain physics, avoiding floating or sliding.

Techniques for Blending Physics and Animation

- **Constraint-based Blending**:

  - Use joints and constraints to maintain basic character structure during ragdoll motion.

  - Transition to full animation when the character stabilizes.

- **Physics-Driven Targets**:

  - Animations drive targets or goals (e.g., hand position), while physics manages intermediate motion.

- **State Machines and Physics States**:

  - Characters switch between animated states and physics states depending on events (e.g., hit reactions).

Practical Example: Ragdoll Recovery

1. Character is knocked down by force.

2. Full ragdoll physics takes over.

3. When velocities fall below thresholds (object at rest):

   - Start blending ragdoll bones toward a standing animation.

4. Complete the recovery animation and return control to the player.

This approach preserves the physical realism of dynamic impacts while maintaining responsive character control.

Real-time physics continues to grow, expanding beyond rigid simulations into dynamic terrains, responsive vehicles, immersive VR experiences, and hybrid animation systems. The future belongs to engines that can blend accuracy, performance, and creativity — offering players worlds that don't just look alive, but *feel* alive.

Bonus Appendices

The core chapters of this book have provided you with the essential knowledge, practical techniques, and design strategies for building a high-performance C++ physics engine. Now, in these bonus appendices, we'll explore additional tools and resources that will help you write cleaner, faster, and more maintainable code, debug complex simulations, and continue your growth as a physics simulation developer.

These appendices cover modern C++ techniques that are especially relevant for physics engines, practical advice for visualizing and debugging simulations, and a curated list of recommended papers, books, engines, and communities.

Let's start with writing modern, efficient C++ code for physics systems.

Appendix A: Modern C++ Techniques for Game Physics

A.1 Smart Pointers and Memory Safety

Physics engines manage hundreds or even thousands of dynamic objects at runtime. Manual memory management quickly becomes error-prone and dangerous, leading to:

- Dangling pointers

- Memory leaks

- Double-deletion crashes

Modern C++ solves much of this with **smart pointers**:

- `std::unique_ptr`: sole ownership of an object (automatically deleted).

- `std::shared_ptr`: shared ownership across multiple systems (reference counted).

- `std::weak_ptr`: non-owning references (used for safely observing shared objects).

In physics engines:

- Use `std::unique_ptr` for RigidBody and Collider instances owned by the World.

- Use `std::shared_ptr` carefully for joint or constraint references.

Example:

cpp

CopyEdit

```
std::vector<std::unique_ptr<RigidBody>> bodies;


bodies.push_back(std::make_unique<RigidBody>(mass));
```

Tip: Prefer `unique_ptr` unless shared ownership is absolutely necessary — simpler, faster, and safer.

A.2 Move Semantics and Resource Management

Physics engines often involve large objects — rigid bodies, matrices, particle arrays — that must be moved around efficiently.

Modern C++ provides **move semantics** (`std::move`) to transfer ownership without copying:

cpp

CopyEdit

```
RigidBody b = std::move(otherBody);
```

When writing classes like `RigidBody`, provide:

- A **move constructor** and **move assignment operator**.

- Delete the copy constructor if moving is the only valid behavior.

Example move constructor:

cpp

CopyEdit

```cpp
RigidBody(RigidBody&& other) noexcept
    : position(std::move(other.position)),
      velocity(std::move(other.velocity)),
      mass(other.mass) { }
```

Move semantics dramatically improve performance by avoiding expensive deep copies during object insertion into containers or return from functions.

A.3 Templates and Meta-programming for Math Libraries

Physics math is heavily vector- and matrix-driven. Writing math libraries manually for every type and dimension is tedious and error-prone.

Modern C++ templates make math libraries:

- **Generic** (work for float, double, int types)

- **Dimension-independent** (2D, 3D, 4D)

- **Optimized** (via compile-time unrolling, inlining)

Example simple templated vector:

cpp

CopyEdit

```cpp
template<typename T>

struct Vector3 {

    T x, y, z;


    Vector3 operator+(const Vector3& other) const {

        return {x + other.x, y + other.y, z + other.z};

    }

};
```

Advanced meta-programming techniques (e.g., `constexpr` functions, expression templates) allow:

- Compile-time computations

- Lazy evaluation for chained math operations

- Highly optimized math code without runtime cost

185

Libraries like **Eigen**, **glm**, or **DirectXMath** use these ideas extensively.

Tip: When building your own math library, start simple — template later when necessary for flexibility or performance.

Appendix B: Visualizing Physics

B.1 How to Debug Physics Visually

Even the most carefully designed physics system can behave unexpectedly due to:

- Missed collisions

- Misaligned colliders

- Incorrect impulses

- Overlapping contacts

Visual debugging — seeing what's happening internally — is crucial.

Key physics visualizations:

- **Collision shapes** (wireframe boxes, spheres)

- **Contact points** (small markers where bodies collide)

- **Collision normals** (arrows showing impulse directions)

- **Velocities** (lines indicating current motion)

- **Constraint links** (lines connecting jointed bodies)

Drawing these in the game world gives immediate insight into what's going wrong — or right.

B.2 Building Simple Debug Tools (Arrows, Bounding Boxes)

Debug visualization doesn't have to be complicated. You can create simple tools that draw basic shapes:

- **Bounding Box Debugging**:

  - Draw a wireframe box from the min/max AABB points.

- **Velocity Arrows**:

  - From object center, draw an arrow in the direction of velocity.

Example pseudo-code:

cpp

CopyEdit

```
drawLine(body.position, body.position + body.velocity *
scaleFactor, Color::Green);
```

- **Contact Point Markers**:

  - Small sphere or cross at the contact point.

Advanced engines implement toggleable debug layers:

- Press a key to switch between normal rendering and debug rendering.

- Color-code different types of collisions (static vs dynamic, awake vs sleeping bodies).

Building and maintaining these tools saves countless hours when developing or tuning your physics engine.

Appendix C: Recommended Resources

Physics simulation is a deep and evolving field. Continued learning from foundational works, open-source projects, and vibrant communities is key to mastering it.

C.1 Key Research Papers and Books

- **"Game Physics Engine Development"** by Ian Millington
  A practical, step-by-step guide to building your own engine — a must-read.

- **"Real-Time Collision Detection"** by Christer Ericson
  Comprehensive reference for collision algorithms, broad phase, narrow phase, and spatial structures.

- **"Advanced Character Physics"** by Thomas Jakobsen
  A foundational paper (used in games like Hitman) explaining verlet integration and soft body dynamics.

- **"Position Based Dynamics"** by Matthias Müller et al.
  Influential technique for cloth, soft bodies, and real-time constraints in modern physics engines.

- **SIGGRAPH Courses and Papers**
  Every year, SIGGRAPH conference papers publish cutting-edge advancements in real-time physics and animation.

C.2 Open-Source Physics Engines for Study (Box2D, Bullet, PhysX)

Studying real-world engines is invaluable.

- **Box2D** (2D physics engine by Erin Catto)

  - Excellent example of simple, clean, efficient physics code.

  - Highly influential; basis for hundreds of games.

- **Bullet Physics** (3D open-source engine)

  - Full-featured 3D physics.

  - Includes rigid bodies, soft bodies, vehicles, and constraints.

  - Used in games, VR, and robotics.

- **NVIDIA PhysX**

  - Industry-standard engine powering AAA titles.

  - Recently open-sourced for study and use.

By reading through these engines' codebases, you'll gain deep insights into optimization, architecture, and handling real-world complexity.

C.3 Communities, Forums, and Continuing Education

Learning doesn't stop after building your first engine.

Here are places to stay connected:

- **GameDev.net Physics Forum**
  Great for discussing problems, sharing ideas, and learning from experts.

- **r/gamedev (Reddit)**
  Active subreddit with many physics and simulation discussions.

- **SIGGRAPH Courses Archive**
  Access papers, slides, and talks from the world's top graphics and simulation researchers.

- **GDC Vault**
  Talks from game developers sharing real-world lessons building physics systems.

- **GitHub Open-Source Projects**
  Studying other projects teaches invaluable lessons in organization, optimization, and extensibility.

Tip: Always pair theory with practice. Reading papers is powerful — but building, testing, and tweaking real simulations is where mastery happens.

Final Note

You now have a full roadmap — from fundamentals to optimization to advanced systems — for creating your own complete, scalable, and powerful C++ physics engine.

Physics simulation is a blend of math, engineering, creativity, and problem-solving. Every new system you build — every bouncing ball, collapsing tower, flowing river, or climbing avatar — brings virtual worlds one step closer to feeling alive.

Keep experimenting, keep learning, and keep pushing the limits.

The world you build is yours.

www.ingramcontent.com/pod-product-compliance
Lightning Source LLC
LaVergne TN
LVHW022342060326
832902LV00022B/4203